1. Prologue

I have always been one for nostalgia. Going back to those corners from your past that filled your life with joy, with inspiration, with exhilaration, and each one of those events that taught you the meaning of life, that enabled you to smile through all the adversities you faced. Much of who I am today and what I do is shaped by those memories, from afar.

These are memories from my work life, travelling to different parts of India, working with various not-for-profit organisations and engaging in the process of transformative change. I have gone back a bit into the later phase of my academic life to give a bit of context to my journey, and some memories that have inspired me in my professional journey.

Recollecting those memories and narrating them has been a very nostalgic journey. It has brought to life some of those experience that I'd like to cherish forever - and it was like reliving those moments in my virtual space, remembering those days and times, those people and through whom, I began understanding incrementally, the various dimensions of life and society.

This book refers to my experiences in India, dating back to 1985 - something which I started writing down since 2002. Since then, I have had several opportunities of going through a similar experience during my various travels to a number of Asian and African countries, which too, I will be writing about someday !

I do hope you enjoy reading these - and I would very much appreciate your comments, which will be a source of encouragement and inspiration for me.

2. My chosen path

I always wanted a make a career in marketing. And so, I wanted to join one of the Indian Institutes of Management (IIM) – which I could not. The only reason I chose to join the Institute of Rural Management, Anand (IRMA) over the other management institute in Ahmedabad was because of the thrill of living in a hostel. Despite the 'rural' prefix to the management diploma, I was confident of getting around to selling soaps or shampoos or tractors or computers ! Little did I realise then that joining IRMA would change the course of my life. It nearly didn't. I ensured that I took up marketing projects during my study and I also got into a marketing job for selling oil, ghee and assorted waste extracts in the summer of 1985.

But it lasted only till I visited my friend and batch mate, Shankar, a couple of months later, to see the work he was doing with an NGO (non-governmental organisation). I remember it was with great disbelief and a bit of scepticism that I received the news of my best friend joining the gang of *'jhola-wallas'* (a term used with some derision to describe those working in NGOs, as we had seen many of them dressed very casually with cloth bags hanging down their shoulders)! But what I thought would be a pleasure trip to Netrang (in South Gujarat where Shankar worked), turned out to be a turning point in my career and life.

"Get into IRMA, become a rural manager, and see how much of respect you will get and how satisfying your work will be" was what Ramu (my friend during my undergraduate days) told me while coaxing me to seriously consider applying for admission to IRMA. I remember my close friend, Sanju and I smirking at Ramu's 'wisdom'. Seeing Shankar in action made

2

Ramu's words ring true. I don't know about the 'respect' part, but he certainly was immensely happy, for he could see how he was able to change the life of village communities so early on in his life.

My mind was made. Five months later, Anil Shah or Anilbhai as he was popularly known (the former Secretary – Rural Development, Government of Gujarat, who became the first Chief Executive of the Aga Khan Rural Support Programme, India – AKRSP-I) offered me a position in AKRSP(I) after I persisted with him over a couple of months. That was in November 1985.

I have never looked back since then. My work in the social development sector has taken me to different parts of the country, many remote locations. "I love this job since it pays you to see the country", said Ajit, a friend and a former colleague of mine, in a lighter vein. He was very true though. Well, our job did pay us not just to see the country, but to understand the country, its people, its culture, its traditions. Each day brought in new challenges, each day brought with it new learnings. Decades later, it still rings true ! New learnings, new challenges and always, the excitement of Change - that change can happen, that change is happening, for the better, and that change is leading to several lives being transformed !

It was in 1983 during my first field visit to a village in Kheda that I first ventured into the countryside (well, I had been to villages in Kerala before, but then, they are so different and relatively more urban than those in other parts of the country). Later the same year, five of us from IRMA (Shankar, Ashutosh, Apoorva, Sudhir and I), spent 2 months in the rural areas of Raipur district, (in Madhya Pradesh state then, now in the state of Chattisgarh). Those 2 months were both fascinating and inspiring - and I remember vaguely we discussing plans of setting up our own NGO at some point in time, which of course hasn't happened in the past 3 decades and probably never will !

The countryside still fascinates me, not in a development tourist sense, but in the way it has subtly but clearly shown me what the not-so-often recognised 'resilience' of Indian people is, in addition to of course being treated to the best of Indian hospitality and warmth. I have had the opportunity of experiencing the various adversities (though in a limited way) of the communities living in different parts of the country, the various other disadvantages they have had to cope with – of being orphaned, destitute, landless, illiterate, outcasts, bonded, disabled, religious minorities, or just being women.....! But all through, what came out was their strong will to overcome these in their own ways, with little hope in store for them. In many cases though, they did manage to overcome these disadvantages with the support of local NGOs and even some sympathetic government functionaries. It has made me realise ever so often how they are the backbone to the Indian economy. It has made me realise how much better endowed and privileged people like me are, and yet, we seem to be little prepared to face the relatively smaller challenges in our lives !

Later on, in my career, I also had the opportunity of visiting many other countries in Asia and Africa. The contexts may be very different, but the underlying issues are often, and depressingly so, very common - the same form of patriarchy, socio-political institutional apathy, discrimination, victimisation, denial of basic entitlements, all of which contribute to growing inequalities in the countries and globally. But yet, community after community also comes up with amazing resilience, of undying spirit to overcome the various challenges - much of which is inspiring and motivating !

It is not only in villages. My work has taken me to various urban settlements of very poor and disadvantaged people. Wanting to escape the hopelessness in their villages, many of them come to cities, attracted by its glitter and promise, but only to lead an even more miserable existence. And one can

4

only be amazed by their resilience and spirit to continue to live on in squalor, leading inhuman lives - and perhaps a bit surprised at the apathy of millions of much better endowed people who mill around them all the time, and whose daily lives of comfort and luxyry depend on them, but completely ignore them or deny their very existence !

I do not wish to romanticise or trivialise these issues. What I'd like to do is to dig into my memories of the past three decades and bring to the fore positive, eventful incidents that make me realise how fortunate I have been in doing what I am and bringing to the fore interesting anecdotes that made my work and times exciting, rewarding and memorable. Possibly, this will paint a picture which is bright and colourful, despite the several adversities that confront the people I met, but who have taken on these challenges as a way of their life and who, in their own way, have enriched lives of occasional visitors like me who often intruded into their lives and yet being so open and welcoming about that ! And therein lies hope and optimism - that these myriad challenges can be overcome with that spirit and courage, backed with a little external support, by millions of disadvantaged people around the world. There are no path breaking revelations, nor do I propose to break any new ground on development thinking. This is, simply put, my recollection of experiencing life the way I did as a social development professional and a tribute to all those people who shared a slice of their life story with me or who enabled me to experience a tiny fraction of their lives − straight from the heart !

I have equally been very fortunate to meet and work with so many inspiring colleagues and friends, whose guidance and motivation was so immensely valuable. The charismatic Anilbhai of AKRSP (I) was my first development guru. Bro. James Kimpton, the British missionary, who chose to spend over seven decades his life in Sri Lanka and India in the service of the poor, showed me what commitment and dedication meant. I worked with his organisation, Reaching the Unreached (RTU) in rural Tamil Nadu. Salil Shetty was

5

and continues to be my source of inspiration, with his amazing enthusiasm for change and his vision of a more equal world. And of course, Shankar Narayanan, who, in addition to being my best friend, is a strong moral supporter and peer, always motivating and encouraging me.

There are scores of colleagues with whom I worked with, in AKRSP(I), RTU, ActionAid, Plan International, the Department for International Development, UK (DFID) and WaterAid, and with those in many of the organisations we partnered with. Over the decades, many of them are now very close friends who continue to encourage, motivate and inspire me. To all of them, my very sincere gratitude for being part of this amazing mosaic of memories. And to all those in the communities I engaged with over this period who were ever so welcoming and ever so positive ! And finally, to my family who were there to support me and (occasionally) listening to my stories !

3. Of living in rural India

It was during the winter in 1982. I was in Anand, a small, sleepy town of Gujarat in western India then, but certainly a bustling town when I last visited in August 2018. I had to appear for an interview, on clearing the written admission test for the Institute of Rural Management - Anand (IRMA), which offered a Post-graduate Diploma in Rural Management (PGDRM). The sight of the lush green campus enthused me, coming from a dry and dusty city of Ahmedabad. The interview panel consisted of 5 members of its faculty.

One of them, the only woman on the panel, was Rajeshwari Rao. She started off with her first question, "What do you know of life in rural India"? Now that was a tough question. I had never seen rural India before. All my knowledge of life in a village was based on my once-in-two-years sojourn to my native Kerala in south India. But then, villages in Kerala are not quite like villages in other parts of the country. Or so I thought ! My other source of information on villages was thanks to Bollywood, with films "*Mera Gaon, Mera Desh*" or "*Sholay*" and I thought villages were probably full of beautiful belles with those enticing backless *cholis* (blouses) or dacoits with rifles riding on horses, where there were endless fairs around temples and where everyone wore colourful dresses, sang and danced all the time, even when performing the most mundane of chores.

But then obviously, that was not the answer that I could give Rajeshwari Rao, much as I wanted to get admission to IRMA. So I said something that I thought was pretty innocent and straightforward, "Oh ! Life in the rural India ? Well, it is about cocks crowing in the morning and cows mooing, where there are beautiful mud huts and a nice pond". I am not kidding. That's exactly what I said – just cannot imagine that I said it then, so naïve was I in my understanding of rural India, at a time when I was hoping to get into rural management ! Of course, I was only nineteen then, so not too worldly wise.

Now I suppose that must be the type of answer that many of the potential candidates gave, or would have given, and still possibly give, year after year. Which is why, during our first term at IRMA, there was a 2-day village orientation visit. But then, this visit was to a village in Kheda district of Gujarat, one of the most prosperous districts of India with very high levels of agriculture and milk production, dominated by the enterprising Patel community. We didn't really get to understand rural India, but yes, we did get to see the co-operative milk society function, which had a larger than life presence. Even the local buses and shops were willing to trade in the coupons as currency, issued by the milk co-operatives in lieu of change, for shortage of small change was quite common.

The women, to the disappointment of many of us guys (and all of us were in our twenties, pretty fresh faced as well), were not as gorgeous as the Asha Parekhs and the Rekhas who normally played the roles of village damsels with great aplomb in many a Bollywood films.

Soon after, we were shown 'Manthan', a film almost like a documentary yet with some of the twists and turns of a mainstream movie that made the narrative very compelling and with a fabulous music score, made on the success of the White Revolution through the dairy co-operatives that made India one of the leading producers of milk and dairy products. Now that film provided some real insights into life in rural India. It was not the gorgeous women-dacoits on horses-village fairs formula film. It was about solidarity at the community level, about the resolve of women and about how village communities were capable enough to bring in an economic revolution. We now felt better informed. It was getting more real !

But then, the real education on life in rural India came a few months later when, in December 1983, the entire batch of about 60 students trooped to various parts of the country in small groups of 4-6 students to spend 2 months in a rural area. It was all quite exciting. We had formed groups amongst ourselves based on common interest and friendship that had been developed over the past 5 months.

The group that I was in, wanted to go to the state of Madhya Pradesh. We had a choice of Jabalpur and Raipur districts. We opted for Raipur, which then was part of Madhya Pradesh. It was an enjoyable 36 hours' train journey by Howrah Express from Ahmedabad to Raipur. The group consisted of Shankar, Ashutosh, Apoorva, Sudhir and myself. We also had a sixth member, Pradeep, who had made it clear to us fairly early on that he just wanted to get into a group but then we should not expect him to be actually part of our group. He was more keen to spend time with his friends in Nagpur which was nearly 300 kilometres away, provided we covered up for him. That was okay by us since he was never an integral part of our group though we were quite fond of him and envied his street smartness. And we needed a sixth guy anyway so that we could be evenly split in groups of 2 to spend time in 3 different villages of Tilda block of Raipur, about 60 kilometres from the district headquarters. The logistics support was to come from the Raipur Milk Union, who had organised basic staying and food arrangements for us in the 3 villages – Tarashiv, Kesda and Bhilodi.

The first two days in Raipur were quite exciting. Five guys in their early twenties in a new city (so what if it was Raipur which was for many of us quite an obscure city in those days?). We started exploring the popular hang-out joints which included the ubiquitous India Coffee House with turbaned waiters in white starched dresses and a couple of cinema halls. The mode of transport was cycle rickshaw. It was difficult for us to fit into one rickshaw. So it was *"ek mein teen, ek mein do"* (3 in one, 2 in the other). In a way, it was good. It helped in bargaining, since we needed 2 rickshaws. Accounting systems to account for the money we were to spend on common items were devised, based on some basic principles that was a combination of equity and equality principles . Sudhir was to maintain accounts, which suited most of us mostly because none of the others were too keen on it and we all trusted Sudhir as he was considered the most responsible of the lot. That is an impression my father also had. It was my father who had booked our train tickets from Ahmedabad to Raipur. Back in the day, there was no online booking or no travel agents. One had to go personally, queue for hours a few months in advance to get train reservations. My father had the patience and very kindly did the booking for us. But when he saw us, he was not quite convinced that the tickets would be safe with any of us, except Sudhir, which is why he handed over the tickets to Sudhir. "He is the only fellow who seems to be responsible", my father said, obviously discounting his own son's sense of responsibility.

We were still quite excited when a couple of days later, we headed to our respective villages. Sudhir and Shankar were to stay in Kesda, Ashu (poor Ashu, he was alone, but then he really didn't mind) was in Bhilodi. Further down, past the block headquarters of Tilda, was Tarashiv, where Apoorva and I were to stay. It was almost afternoon when we reached our village. Crisp dry winter winds blew, the effect of which was toned down by the afternoon sun. As we got out of the jeep, we took a quick look around. This looked like a real village. Not like the semi-urban look of Kerala villages. Not the prosperous look like the villages of Kheda. A dusty one kilometre path led us from the main road (which an apology of a road, just wide enough to let a vehicle pass, for which all the rest coming from the other direction had to jump off the road, literally, a few feet away and below to avoid a collision). It was not a large village. There were 50-60 houses, many of them thatched. The better looking ones had rounded tiles made locally of earth and heated in a local kiln, supported by a mesh of bamboo poles.

Our first stop in the village was the dairy co-operative, housed in a dingy one room measuring barely 10 feet by 8 feet. A small wooden table, a steel cupboard, four folding chairs and an assortment of measuring vessels was what the co-operative had, a far cry from the *pucca* two-storey building measuring about 2000 square feet that we had seen in Kheda. As true beneficiaries of the White Revolution that was instrumental in giving birth to IRMA, we asked a few quick questions. Milk collection was a measly 20 litres per day, which was considered good, as it could drop down to 10 litres at times. A 20 litres daily collection was respectable enough for that area (abysmal by Kheda standards), for it meant one full can of milk.

The next stop was our home, our home that was to be for the next one month. It belonged to the young secretary of the milk co-operative, Somu, who lived in the house with his parents, his wife and his two children. Our home, or to put it more plainly, the room, was just as big, or probably a shade smaller, than the office of the milk co-operative. It had no windows. It had a door which had to be fastened by a chain that was hooked on to the wall. The door had vertical fissures in it, big enough to let the outside sunlight stream in when it was closed – which was useful, for the room had no window. There was a similar door on the other side of the room, but that opened out to the courtyard of Somu's house. In the corner of the courtyard right outside the rear door of our 'home' was the barn where their two bullocks and two cows (nice bovine couples !) lived. They had been strategically placed behind the rear door of our room, I thought, for it provided them with the support when their foreheads were itchy. Except that it always gave us an eerie feeling that someday they would kick or hit the fragile door open and trample over us. There was only one bed which was a traditional rope cot with wooden frames, just big enough for one person to sleep. The other person had to sleep on the floor. Initially, Apoorva and I took turns at sleeping on the bed, but then he decided that his life was too precious to be trampled under the hoofs of a naive cow or a bullock and so monopolised the bed !

The day time was okay. There was enough sunlight, thanks to the gaps on our door. It gave us the privacy we wanted, because we could close the door and yet ensure that there was enough light in the room. The cows and the bullocks didn't bother us in the day. You see, they had their own sense of decency and were loathe to disturb our afternoon siesta. But then, having granted us that liberty, they would then be liberal in their snorts and farts, grunting with satisfaction every time they urinated loudly or lay their dung. The only other noise they would make was when they shuffled impatiently, kicking with their hooves to keep the flies and mosquitoes at bay. But I am sure they never meant to disturb us. They were far too innocent for that.

But Apoorva would not buy that theory. You see, he had always been brought up in a big city. It was Bombay initially and then Ahmedabad. And before that, he also had a brief London stint. He could barely make out the difference between a cow and a bullock. I was more empowered with my knowledge of cows and bullocks, having seen them at my grandparents' place during my summer vacations in Kerala. But the only thing I found difficult to accept and where I joined ranks with Apoorva was the strange smell in our room. It was a mixture of the body odour of the animals, the dung and urine, the hay and an assortment of cattle feed and of damp earth – partly because we had an earthen floor and partly because of the dampness of the barn behind. So much so that even we started smelling like them, meaning, our bovine friends !

4. The morning rituals in Tarashiv

The first day in Tarashiv, our chosen village, was pretty okay. This was way back in December 1983 when Apoorva and I were to spend a month in this village as part of our rural orientation, which, in turn, was as part of our rural management studies. We didn't have anything to do. We

12

walked around a little bit to get to know the lanes. There were not very many, anyway, so it didn't actually need much time. The houses were in neat little rows facing each other. In the evening, we went to the milk co-operative, in time for the evening collection, of milk hoping to be of some help. The secretary, our landlord, was there, waiting for people to come and pour their milk. The people were coming in a trickle, with milk in bottles and small utensils. They didn't have much to contribute to the pool anyway. No single contribution had exceeded a litre, a far cry from the Kheda co-operatives in Gujarat, where there used to long queues of people, mostly women, to pour milk, after which they would move to another queue to collect their cash payment for the previous day's milk and after which they stood in yet another queue, some of them, to buy cattle feed. So it meant on their way back, they (mostly women) would have an empty brass pot or big steel utensils with a long handle, all empty, a kilo or two of processed, nutritious cattle feed and still have enough money to take back home as hard cash, in their fists or tucked away into their blouses or in a cloth purse that would hang around their waist.

However, none of this was required in Tarashiv. Cash could be available only once a week, or if the Raipur (district level) dairy was going through a liquidity problem, it could be once a fortnight or even longer. There was no cattle feed stock. In fact, no one bought cattle feed, as no one could afford to. Which then meant that the bullocks were only as big as the cows, the cows looked like calves and the calves were barely bigger than the mongrels that roamed around ! We once came across a family of 17 cows and so, we thought they would be the single largest contributor to the milk society. But that was not the case. They had barely managed to pour 10-15 litres of milk during an entire month as most of the cows were dry and there was only one which gave milk every day, most of which had to be used for home consumption !

Coming back to our first day in Tarashiv, as night approached, the winds got a little chilly. Our landlord, the secretary of the milk co-operative, was also the provider of our food. We were never very clear on the terms. We weren't told, nor did we ask. The arrangement had been made by the Raipur Milk Union who told us that we would have to pay a 'reasonable amount', though the reasonable amount was not specified. We welcomed the darkness. It helped us to get over the inconvenience of not having access to a toilet. We didn't have to go far to urinate, at least ! Any bush round the corner was fine. Not that we were not used to urinating in the open. It was quite easy in the anonymity that a city like Ahmedabad could offer, where the chance of a person known to you seeing you pee in public would be extremely rare and hence worth taking the risk. Whereas here, on the first day itself, we had been seen and noticed by several people in the village as urban outsiders, a couple of clueless young men, and several more would see us and we had to continue living there for at least a month !

The food was hot and delicious (it was partly because we were very hungry and partly because it was our first meal, not realizing that the menu would largely be unchanged throughout the rest of the month). It consisted of plain white rice (which had a nice aroma - remember, we were in the rice bowl of India, Chattisgarh) in a heap in a round *thali* (plate) and *dal* (lentils) made of green grams. Yes, we did look at the *dal* very carefully. Those were the days when there was a raging controversy on the after effects of regular use of the saffron-coloured *(kesar) dal* which was commonly consumed in Raipur and the neighbouring districts (which now form the state of Chhattisgarh). It was said that regular consumption of *kesar dal* could lead to paralysis. Though the local people couldn't care less, for us, we did not want to take a chance. Hence the sight of a green gram *dal* was very welcome. There was also a little vegetable (this would change regularly, but normally it was potatoes and aubergine).

It had been a long day. A 60 kilometres ride by jeep from Raipur, settling in our new home, walking round the village, an evening at the milk co-operative – well certainly, our insulated carefree life on the IRMA campus with its idyllic setting had not prepared us for something more taxing ! We snuggled into our beds, one on the bed, one on the floor. And while we were dying to sleep (we actually went to sleep at 8.30 p.m., again, a far cry from our sleeping time at IRMA, which was never before 2.00 a.m.!), we found ourselves tossing and turning around.

For me, it was possibly because it was a new place. But then there were other factors too. The excitement of being in a new place, the slight discomfort at the complete silence all around, except for the grunting noises that our bovine neighbours made occasionally, worrying sick about the possibility of having to share the floor with snakes or scorpions or other insects.....! For Apoorva, it was almost entirely to do with the threat of the cows knocking down the rear door and trampling him or goring him, depending upon where and how they caught him ! He cursed the cows each time the thought about them disturbed him, cursed himself for choosing to come to a village and stay in a place where the cows could just walk it with little effort with their threatening horns and hooves, cursed himself for having joined IRMA and having to undergo such unusual travails, far from the comforts of his home in Ahmedabad ! But somehow, we managed to sleep.

We kept hearing various sounds and noises from early in the morning, but it was too early for us to wake up. 8 a.m. was normally a reasonable time to wake up while we were on the IRMA campus as classes started at 9 a.m. and so we had thought we will give up an hour's sleep and wake up at 7 a.m. instead. With every passing moment, the sounds and noises became louder. People talking, the heavy metal handle of the buckets hitting the rim as women poured water into the various brass pots they had collected from the village well, the creaking sound of men's footwear as they untied the cows and led them to wherever they intended to take them, of sounds and smells from the kitchen and so on. And yes, the cocks crowing (well, they kept on crowing endlessly even after they would have managed to wake up the entire village !) and the cows mooing, calling out for either getting their udders emptied or to draw attention to their empty stomachs. 7 a.m. still seemed quite early in the morning, for we had no work to do, no classes to attend. All that we had to do was understand and observe life in rural India and then write about it.

We came out to the veranda and started brushing our teeth. It must have seemed a strange sight to those who walked past, seeing us brush in a very strange manner with white froth forming at the corners of our mouth. Most of the people we saw had a neem twig which they kept on chewing while they went about their other errands – herding their cattle, carrying wood and haystacks on their heads, cycling down the road. Some were, like us, stationed at one place while they rubbed their teeth vigorously with the *kala dant manjan* – the black tooth powder, which was locally made and commonly used in several parts of rural India. We even had it in Kerala. It was called '*mukkeri*' in my mother tongue, Malayalam. In cities, they came in neat little and for some reason, red coloured packets. I remember, in Ahmedabad, one of the most popular brands was the 'Monkey' brand. Later on, these were replaced by Dabur's *lal* (red) *dant manjan* and the Colgate's white tooth powder. Not to forget the ayurvedic Vicco Vajradanti (whoever bought them ? But their ads were all over the place, from posters to cinemas!).

So far, so good ! But then, the rumbling in our stomachs started. It was time to answer the nature's call. For some reason we were quite optimistic to find a toilet, but did not quite know how to go about identifying one. Just as we were wondering about asking our landlord, his mother came out and handed over a steel *lota* to us which could just about hold a litre of water, "*Yeh bahar jaane ke liye hai*" (This is for you for going 'out' - 'out' being a euphemism for toilet, which we did not know at that time). We did not quite understand what that meant, for we hadn't asked for one. But then, the *lota*, in addition to being symbolic for various other things, was also symbolic of the morning (or the evening) ablutions ! Fortunately, we were carrying with us a plastic mug too, so that we did not have to be sequential about answering the calls of nature, the longer one, that is, as it was one *lota* for the two of us ! "You can fill the water from the pond which is on the way to the fields", Somu said helpfully.

It was a cold morning. Our rubber *chappals* (slip-ons) were not good enough to keep our feet from freezing. But our pressing need and the anxiety of finding a good enough place to let it all out on our first day in the village (we had overeaten the whole of the previous day in Raipur, considering the fact that urban food would now be a month away) made us tread gingerly on the path that led us out of the village to the pond where many like us were visible. They seemed to have completed their task as we could see them wash their hands.

We didn't have the faintest idea where we needed to go and how far we needed to go. We hadn't bothered to check it out with Somu. We thought of walking as far away as possible. As we made our way through the freshly ploughed farms that grew pulses, over the lumps of damp earth, our feet started freezing even more with the fresh cold dew that was very visible on the plants and wild grass. And as our need became more pressing, we started walking faster, awkwardly negotiating over the lumps of damp earth in our most unsuitable *chappals* (no wonder those who wore footwear chose to wear a very rigid sort of a leather *chappals*). The now-less-than-a-litre water from our plastic mug and *lota* started spilling miserably, drastically reducing the quantity of this precious liquid that would ensure our hygiene !

Finally, we came to the corner of a farm with a nice protective hedge all around. "This place looks safe" said Apoorva in great relief. And just as we were about to go onto our haunches, we saw someone coming straight across the farm from behind the very hedge which we thought would give us privacy ! And before he could notice us, we darted to the other side of the hedge, looking for a safer place. It took a good five more minutes to identify the next safest place. This time, we said enough was enough. We could not hold on any longer. And if someone did see us in the act, well, there was no choice. So there we were, out in the open on a cold morning in Tarashiv, delightfully relieving ourselves, happy at the thought that our act of commission would make someone's farm organically more rich !

This was the first time I was going out in the open. Not that I was used to attached toilets all my life. In the government quarters that we stayed in Ahmedabad, the toilet was in our backyard, a good 10 feet away from our living space. That was okay except on freezing winter early mornings, when we had to go to school early in the morning, twice a week on a Wednesday and a Saturday. As a kid, the cold and the dark were ingredients for a certain mortal fear, till I was about 7 or 8. Our village in Kerala was different. At least, till the seventies, the toilet was about 40 feet away from the house, in the midst of our 'parambu' or the open land dotted with coconut palms and various other trees that was typical of most houses in the country side. There were two neighbouring houses. One belonged to my great grandmother and the other to my grandaunt, both on the maternal side. One was a *pucca* one, the other, a *kutcha* one. The *pucca* one was pretty much like the typical Indian ones that you would see in a government quarters, like the one we lived in, except that there was no water tap. Instead, there was a water tank into which we had to pour water drawn from the well. The *kutcha* one was made of sheets of coconut leaves woven into mats which provided for an enclosure without a door. You had to turn in left to enter it and then turn right to get to the place where you would perform your job. It didn't have a septic tank. It had a pit. You had to squat on the two wooden planks while you relieved into the pit. To avoid looking below, one would look up at the heads of the swaying palms, which made for a much better sight and also enabled you to keep the nose turned up. I would avoid this structure as much as possible. I was most worried that someone would barge in while I was there and hence keep on coughing incessantly to keep the potential trespassers away.

Coming back to Tarashiv, the most anxious moments, especially in the early days, was about finding a safe place to relieve ourselves. Thankfully, I found Apoorva more fastidious than me. By the time he has scouted around for a suitable place with his own security checks to make sure that he could get his 10 minutes of peace to complete his job, I would have done mine. And it was this type of pressure that made us alter our waking up timing. We were now up at 6 a.m. in the morning to take advantage of the morning winter darkness. Of course, it meant we would encounter more people on our way to or way back from the fields, but the morning darkness lent us a relative anonymity that we welcomed !

5. The letter from Arulmany

Life in Tarashiv continued to be uneventful. Days were short because of the winters. December was coming to an end and we were at the threshold of 1984. The only thing (or so it seemed to me) that made life eventful at all were our occasional visits to the nearest townTilda (which was a glorified village but a buzzing market place), or Kesada or Bhiladi where our friends Shankar, Sudhir and Ashu were based, or the more regular evening waits by the roadside in the dark for the milk collection van to bring us letters from our friends. Our batchmates from IRMA where we were doing our rural management course, were spread across many states for our mandatory 2 months rural orientation.

Letters from friends describing how they were getting along in their respective rural environments were pretty interesting and insightful. But the one that took the cake was the one we received from Arulmany who was in Erode, Tamil Nadu. This was soon after the New Year, in early January. He was writing this letter soon after one of the faculty members, Srinivas, had just stayed with him for a couple of days on one of the routine visits that the faculty did while the students were in the field. Srinivas was a relatively new member of the faculty and this was probably his first rural visit and stay. Having graduated from one of the elite Indian Institutes of Management in India and teaching Financial Management, poor Srini (as he was fondly referred to) may never have expected to undergo this kind of an experience ! Arulmany's letter went something like this (this is not an actual reproduction, but a recollection from memory) :

" Having Srini around was great fun. You know what a simple, nice and shy fellow he is ! He was quite cool and we had a good time. His only problem was going to the toilet. We didn't have one. On the day he arrived, he asked me where the toilet was. I said there was no toilet. He was horrified. What do you do then, he asked. We go out in the open, I said. But where, he asked. This place is full of houses. We do to the side of the road, I said. But then there is so much traffic passing by, he said. But I said, there is no choice. When does the traffic stop, he asked. I said, the last bus passes by at 11.30 p.m. Ok then, I will go only after that, he said. But what will you do till then, I asked. I will hold on, he said.

So, he would wait till it was night. I would then escort him through the lanes to keep an eye on the snakes that could be around and about which, Srini was scared stiff. When we came up to the road, he would find a suitable place to squat and then ask me to switch off the torch, while he went about his business. On the second day too, the same thing happened. I sat up till late and after 11.30 p.m., escorted Srini to the road which was a little distance away.

At the appointed place across the road, Srini sat down and asked me to switch off the torch. I was on the other side of the road. I switched it off. And while I looked around gazing at the stars, enjoying the cool night breeze and listened casually to the sound of insects around me, I heard Srini ask, 'Arulmany, what is the time' ? 'Can I switch on the torch to check'? I asked. 'Ok, but turn the other way and switch it on. I am not finished as yet', he said. I turned around and switched on the torch to check my wrist watch. It was five minutes past twelve. 'It is 12.05, Srini', I said. 'Thanks Arulmany. Wish you a Happy New Year', came his reply. That's how I welcomed the new year this time ! Hope you guys had a better way of celebrating the new year!"

6. The goodbye

It was March 1985. We were preparing for a new phase in our lives. We were the fourth batch of students to graduate with a Post Graduate Diploma in Rural Management from IRMA. It had been a memorable and fun filled two years. While we learnt about becoming good managers, most of us will remember our time in IRMA even more for the bonding and the fun that we as a batch of nearly 60 students had during our two years. The three stints of assignments outside the campus (one 'fieldwork' and two 'Management Traineeship Segment' or MTS) got us in smaller groups working on specific projects. After each of those stints which lasted a couple of months each, we all were eager to come back and share our experiences, but also to catch up with our friends who we sorely missed. And in those days without mobiles, emails or Facebook, it was difficult to be in touch.

Our convocation was on March 15th 1985, before which we all were going through our campus recruitments. From the first week of March itself, some of us were successful in getting jobs that we wanted. Some of us had planned for a short holiday before we commenced our working careers. But after March 15th, most of us had plans to start leaving the very next day – except myself. I was waiting for an opening with the Sikkim Milk Federation and they were meant to come only on March 18th for the recruitment. There were a couple of others who were to be around on March 17th, but most of my batch mates left by March 16th.

It was quite an emotional period for us. The mood was sombre and it certainly overtook the excitement of getting our diplomas and launching ourselves into our careers. Packing our bags and disposing off unwanted stuff had started in right earnest. Since many of us were expecting our parents, siblings and friends to come for the convocation by March 13 or 14, we

22

wanted to scrub our rooms clean, keep it tidy and get ready to leave from the evening of March 15th.

I had to travel only a short distance, of 70 kilometres to Ahmedabad and hence, I did not need much time to prepare for my departure. My parents, sister and two of my close friends were coming for the convocation on March 14th and they were to leave soon after. And since I had to stay on till March 18th, I had plenty of time to pack. Hence, I instead spent time in helping many of my friends to pack and clear their rooms. In many cases, I borrowed the bicycle from Sagar, the manager of our canteen, cycled down to Jagnath which was a couple of kilometres away to get an auto rickshaw, helped people get their belongings loaded into the auto rickshaws, and together with other friends, made our way to the railway station to see off our friends. Those last few moments on the campus were precious and we wanted to make use of each one of those as we knew we could never ever get back to that setting in our entire lives – certainly not with this group !

The last of my friends left by the evening of March 16th. It was quite a long and forlorn journey back from the railway station that I made to IRMA. The hostel was quiet. Though our junior batch was around, most of them were in separate hostel blocks. The silence was killing. I was missing my friends terribly. Shankar, Naushad, Vikram, Ashu and Sudhir had planned a trip to Goa. I had to miss the trip since I was waiting for the Sikkim Federation recruitment. But then at least I did look forward to meeting them a few days later in Bangalore – so there was something to look forward to. But even that was not enough to cheer me as I spent some long, lonely hours on the campus. And to make matters worse, I was informed, on March 17th, that the Sikkim Federation had pulled out of the recruitment and that they were not coming ! That was quite a blow.

So, on March 17th, I decided to pack my bags and leave early morning on March 18th. After having helped many of my friends with their packing, I was quite dejected that I had to do it all myself. After having gone and fetched an auto rickshaw for many of my friends and having seen them off at the railway station, I dreaded at the prospect of having to do it all myself. I was slipping into a state of self pity, feeling quite sorry for myself that there will be no one to see me off, at the campus or at the railway station. All my friends had left. And even though I had a few friends from the junior batch, 6.30 a.m. was too early a time for anyone to bother waking us just to say good bye to me !

In the evening, I made a round to the boys' hostel to meet some of my friends from the junior batch and wish them good bye. A little later, I went to the girls' block (the A Block) to meet a few girls and say good bye to them as well – there were 3-4 girls who were good friends and I wanted to meet them before I left.

I went to her room last. As I knocked, she opened the door. "I just came to say good bye. I am leaving tomorrow morning", I said. "But then why are you saying good bye now if you leaving only tomorrow" ? she asked. "Well, I will be leaving early". "How early" ? " 6.30 in the morning", I replied. "Oh, then there is plenty of time. See you at dinner", she said with a smile and that trademark twinkle. "Well, that's it", I thought. I had said good byes to all that I need to say and it was now time to go for dinner and then get back to packing. I needed to be up early in the morning.

I woke up at 5 a.m. in the morning. After a quick shower and change, I went to the canteen to collect the bicycle keys from Sagar and made by way to Jagnath. It was a crisp spring morning with the sun shining radiantly. The campus looked even more beautiful. The lawns even more green. I just did not want to leave the place. But the sense of loneliness after all my friends had departed was too strong and I just could not bear to be there on my own any longer. I had to leave. I could have taken a later train, but that was enough. I had to leave and wanted to leave. At Jagnath, I hailed an auto rickshaw and asked the driver to follow me to the hostel blocks while I rode ahead of him.

Once back in the hostel, I quickly parked the bicycle in front on the canteen, handed over the keys to the cook, ran up the steps to my room on the second floor of the C block and starting bringing my bags down – three in all, one big suitcase, which I brought down first and loaded into the auto rickshaw and went running back to get the 2 small bags. Taking the bags out and one final look into the room that had been my home for 2 lovely years and one final glance down the corridors of C Top (as we fondly referred it as), I made my way down the stairs, looked towards what had been Naushad's room, and then came down and paused a bit in front of Shankar's room, the hub of C Block, now eerily quiet and came out of the block, not turning back, but with my head down, walking straight towards the auto rickshaw. "That's it", I told myself. "This is now really the end of my life in IRMA".

As I turned around the C block and past the D block to where the auto rickshaw was waiting, to my utter surprise and delight, I saw her, standing by the auto rickshaw, looking radiant in her bright red dress, her dupatta casually around her neck, hands folded, looking towards me with the same twinkle in her eye and the smile ! "Look, I told you last evening that it was too early to say good bye". I was overwhelmed. A range of emotions crossed my mind. "Why did you take the trouble"? I asked her. "Trouble ? What trouble ? I just wanted to. And I knew that there wouldn't be anyone to say good bye to you. Good bye and good luck ! Let's keep in touch", she said. All that I managed was a rather inaudible "Thank you", a nod, a smile and a wave. I got into the auto rickshaw, looked out and waved out to her. The auto rickshaw made a noisy start, spewing out fumes that seemed to jerk me back to reality of what was an unusual morning. As the auto rickshaw turned away from the block, I looked back towards the hostel blocks through the opening at the back of the vehicle. With a final wave, she had turned back, walking back to her room.

Words cannot explain what I felt at that time. It was a feeling of immense gratitude, of being overwhelmed and being completely humbled by her gesture. And that is why, several years later, it is still so vivid in my mind. Today, she leads a contented life in Delhi with her husband and son. After a stint of working with NGOs, she has turned a writer. She has already published a few books and speaks at various literature festivals and events. She remains as warm and humane as she always was. And innumerable friends of her, like myself, remember her for what she was and is. She is Daman.

7. Magan of Sapar

It was in March 1986 that the work of renovating the Sapar
(Surendranagar district, Gujarat) percolation tank started. I
was working with the Aga Khan Rural Support Programme –
India (AKRPS-I), an NGO, that worked on developing natural
resources for improving the livelihoods of the poor.
Surendranagar was one of the 3 districts chosen, as it was
perennially affected by droughts, sometimes for 3-4
consecutive years.

The renovation of the Sapar tank was part of a drought relief
programme that AKRSP-I had taken up largely with
government funding. There was a series of meetings with the
people of Sapar and Brahmapuri villages who were to work on
this site. We kept insisting that it should and would be
different from the government sponsored works in the sense
that their rights as workers would be respected and that they
would be encouraged to take responsibility of ensuring
equitable access to employment opportunities.

These were, as readers may recall, the early days of
participatory development and various NGOs at that time
were experimenting with their own understanding of
'participation'. Most of the meetings were in the late evenings.
Children invariably outnumbered adults (read, men) in these
meetings, but were often shooed away with "This is none of
your business, go away" type of remarks. Not the ones to be
deterred, they would faithfully reassemble, a little away from
the adults, curious, huddled in groups, trying to understand
what was happening.

The boys were expectedly more boisterous, trying to imitate
their adults by tying a towel around their heads like a turban,
leaning carelessly against the wall, and in turn, shooing off the
girls with a similar "This is none of your business..." type of

27

statements. The girls, not to be left behind would still reassemble, a little farther away from the boys, whispering excitedly, pulling their *odhnis* (a colourful length of fabric that the girls started wearing from their adolescence which was loosely wrapped round their shoulders and with which they would cover their heads).

It was in one such meeting that the inauguration of the work was announced for the following day. Eight in the morning was the time decided. About 30 people – 20 from Sapar and 10 from Brahmapuri were to come and start working. The wages were announced (which was as per the wage rates announced by the government for drought relief works) and other related conditions of employment on the site were explained. A local committee agreed to make a list of those eligible for the first round of employment.

It was one of the first major projects the AKRSP-I staff team was undertaking since they set up their Surendranagar office in April 1985. With great enthusiasm, the entire team made their way to the site with coconuts and *agarbattis* (incence sticks) being more conspicuous than measure tapes and technical maps. As with any such important work, the ceremonial rituals to invoke divine blessings and ensure that work would progress without any hassles were considered auspicious and drilled into our psyche. By 8 am, the team was there (which was rather unusual), with a beaming Bharatbhai, the big built gentle giant engineer with a booming voice (who was on secondment from the state government), proceeding to the place where the work was to start. But strange enough, there was not a soul was in sight. None of the committee members, none of the supposedly identified 'first round workers' were in sight.

We climbed on to the tank *bund* (the earthen wall of the tank) to look at Sapar on the right and Brahmapuri on the left to see if we could see anyone coming. There was no one in sight. As we got down and decided to wait, we saw someone climbing over the *bund* and heading in our direction. We could distinctly make out the spade and a *tagara* (used for carrying loose earth). "Finally, one of the workers" we said, delighted. The bright yellow shirt and the brown trousers were also distinctly visible, and so was the pink towel wrapped around his head like a turban. It did not take us long to realise that it was Magan, one of the most enthusiastic of the boys from the Koli Patel community (which was one of the dominant communities in these villages in terms of numbers), a 15-year old from a poor family that could not afford to send him to school.

Life as a daily wage labourer had toughened him. He had started working earlier on in life. His palms were hard with years of working with the spade and the plough. His frame though lean, was tough and muscular. He had often expressed his desire, rather ruefully, to go to school, but it had never happened. It was rare to see him idle. If it was not work on the farm or a construction site, it was grazing the cows or fetching water – but always someone who welcomed us with a bright smile, ready to run around to muster the adults for a village meeting whenever required.

" Bharatbhai, I am ready. Can I start work"? he asked with his usual cheerful smile. On being asked about the others, he simply said "They will come, but can I start ? Because you are going to pay me piece rate wages. The more I work, the more I'll earn. And I can work faster, earlier in the day". We were in a bit of dilemma about engaging a 'child labourer'. We were new on this job and hence did not know what to do. "The government rules prohibit anyone under 14. He is 15, so it is ok", announced Bharatbhai. The decision was made. Magan started work by hitting the spade on the ground at a place he was allotted and put the earth into the *tagara,* amidst applause from all of us. He was delighted.

That was the beginning of our friendship. The work on the site went on regularly for almost 4 months. At its peak, there were 550 people working on the site at any given point in time. But on each of my visits to the site, it was pleasure to look out for him, to be greeted cheerfully by him and occasionally, accompany him back to the village, while he narrated the events of the day. He was one of the most regular workers on the site and took back a tidy sum each week. He was an example in dedication for all those on the site. Someone even nicknamed him 'engineer *saheb* (sir)', since he was seen assisting the site supervisor, often out of his own interest and curiosity in taking measurements of the work done and even supervising the work with the site supervisor, walking along the 2 kms earthen *bund*. Summer had set in. Temperatures went soaring to an average of 42 degrees Celsius. It was dry all around, and even as people struggled to keep up with the intemperate weather and shield themselves every now and then from the heat, Magan went around his work meticulously without any hint of tiredness or physical exhaustion ! When asked about how he could keep up with the work in these conditions, he answered simply with a smile, "I have got used to this" !

I kept in touch with him till 1988. He must have now grown up into a responsible, caring and a strong man, and I hope, with his commitment to his family and village still very deep, as he had demonstrated at such a young age !

8. Chandrelia's Jeevan and Malla

A few months after we met Magan, we met another boy of a similar age but from a totally different background. Jeevan was the son of Merubhai, the Koli (a 'backward class' Hindu community) village headman of Chandrelia in Surendranagar district, Gujarat. A small time contractor, Merubhai was relatively prosperous by local standards, owning a tractor and a reasonable patch of agriculture land. A small time politician to the core, he spent substantial time bowing to the powers-that-be, which included the local politicians, the bureaucrats, the influential village elders.....well, just about anyone who could ensure that a small contract comes his way, so much so that he had perennially got into this very deferential habit, with his head half-bowed, hands folded respectfully and a rather indulgent type of hospitality – none of which went down well with our colleague, Shashi, (or 'Havsibhai' as he was referred to in the villages and known for his direct, no-nonsense approach, who was responsible for overseeing work in a cluster of villages that included Chandrelia), who found Merubhai's sycophancy disgusting, difficult to handle and always was suspicious of him. In fact, the very sight of Meru irked Shashi, almost to the point of angering him.

Jeevan was quite a contrast, and that is what attracted us to him. A boy quite tall for his age, he would be eager to come and chat with us, look at our writing pads, play around with our pen, question us about our work with an ease and confidence that did not go quite well with his father who felt that he was taking too much of liberty with the 'Aga Khan saheb-log (officers)' !. It used to be quite a strange sight at times – Merubhai, sitting on the floor in front of us, shoulders bent, respectfully, refusing to sit beside us on the wooden cot he would have laid out, while Jeevan sitting right next to us and interacting with us without any inhibition.

As a teenager and that too, from a relatively better off family in a small village of about 40 households, Jeevan commanded the respect of his peers and children younger than him. They looked up to him because he could write, utter a few words in English, felt free to talk to us like a friend would. He could also read and write (which few other children could), rode a bicycle and even knew how to drive a tractor ! And Jeevan befriending us meant that the other children (well, boys only, of course, as girls had to stay away !) also became our friends.

Soon, we started having regular meetings with the group of boys under Jeevan's 'leadership'. It was so refreshingly different from dealing with difficult adults ! Talking to them about anything under the sun was great fun. They also wanted to do some work to 'develop' their village. That was the time our colleague, Depinder, was engaged in the social forestry project on public wastelands. We hence talked to the kids about planting fruit trees in front of their homes and caring for them, an idea they jumped on ! The seedlings were given to Jeevan who then took personal responsibility to not just distribute these equally, but also to monitor its growth. He would proudly show us a notebook which he referred to as his 'register' and with great importance, towel wrapped around his neck, his ink stained fingers holding a pen, would walk around the village, checking each sapling and marking a tick against the name of the child who was responsible for that tree. And all that the children got in return was an approving nod from their 'leader' !

In spite of us being a fairly common sight in the village, not many children were comfortable talking to us on a one-to-one basis, unless prompted by Jeevan or an adult from their family or community. But one of them, Malla, came out of his shell eventually.

A 11-year old, he belonged to the Vanjara community (traditional nomadic group, who were gradually settling down in permanent habitations). His family was headed by his widowed mother, Buriben, a young, articulate woman, with a great degree of self-confidence and self-esteem, who had decided to bring up Malla and his younger sister by herself, working on her small farm, without depending on anyone else. Malla was constantly beside her, helping her with the ploughing, weeding, grazing and everything else than a young man from a farming community would be expected to do. Naturally, he could not go to school, having had to drop out soon after his father's untimely death. Kana, the head of the Vanjaras and a close pal of Meru, and the rest of his community were also not too helpful to Buriben and her children, though they were one of the poorest families in the village.

Fortunately, Buriben was noticed in one of the meetings which was held to identify those who would raise a nursery of seedlings for the social forestry project. While Buriben went around raising one of the best nurseries that year with ruthless efficiency, it was the pride on Malla's face that was truly worth noticing. We just had to visit the nursery each time we went there, for Malla had put in immense amount of work alongside his mother. In addition, Malla was also part of Jeevan's group of youngsters and one of the keenest kids in raising fruit trees on his homestead. Malla also provided us interesting insights into the small politics in the village as he understood – the rivalry between the Kolis and Vanjaras (in spite of the friendship between their respective leaders, which was obviously to protect their own personal interests), the way his mother was uncared for because of being a widow and many more. But these adversities were not demanding enough to wipe out Malla's smile or his enthusiasm. His dream ? He wanted to own a good patch of irrigated land where he could grow enough crops and trees to feed the family and meet their needs.

Jeevan and Malla would be in their forties now. I keep wondering about the paths they may have chosen. Would they now be leaders or role models for the youth of their respective communities of their villages ? Would they have left the village and taken up work in a city nearby ? I don't know. But what I do feel is that they must be doing pretty well in life. Both had shown a great deal of enthusiasm to what was happening in their village. Both were part of a process of change at a very impressionable age in their lives. Both must have imbibed some valuable principles and lessons in their lives, learning from what they saw happening with such keenness. Or would they ?

9. Ala, the inspiration

Working in Surendranagar district was always a challenge for us in AKRSP -I, especially in the mid to late eighties when, as an organisation, we were still in the process of establishing ourselves and our credibility. Most of the staff were new and most in their early to mid twenties. There were some on secondment from the Gujarat state government. As expected, work ethics and work culture were drastically different between these two groups. These were the early days of 'participation' when Prof. Robert Chambers (from the Institute of Development Studies, Sussex, UK, widely considered to be the guru of participatory approaches) had stared propounding the 'rapid rural appraisal' (or the popularly known RRA) techniques, but this did not resonate much with our government colleagues.

There were several other challenges. A deeply entrenched feudal culture dominated by the powerful *Darbar* community meant that initiating social mobilisation processes was quite a challenge in itself. Tensions between the *Koli Patels* (a so-called backward caste / class group generally agriculturists and labourers) and the *Rabari* (also backward caste/class and traditional cattle herders) communities, especially over cattle grazing and the use of public lands was a contentious issue. Surendranagar was also one of the most drought prone districts of India. While I was with AKPSP-I, I witnessed one of the worst droughts the district had seen, the drought of 1987, which had followed two previous years of droughts, consecutively.

It was in this backdrop that we had made our first forays into Thoriyali, a village near the town of Sayala, the block headquarters, sometime in 1985. Though I can't recollect the exact reasons why we went there, I vaguely recall that it had to do with the rather creditable performance of the village milk co-operative, something that one of my colleagues who came from Anand, the land of AMUL (or the Anand Milk Union Limited), was attracted to as he also worked earlier with the National Dairy Development Board. AMUL was a district level federation of village milk co-operatives, which, through its successful processing and production facilities, became well known for its AMUL brand of milk and milk products and was widely considered a success story globally in co-operative organisation of village level producers, leading to the widely successful 'White Revolution' in India). My own background of having studied rural management in the neighbouring IRMA campus too attracted me to look at the milk co-operative.

Those days, the District Rural Development Agency (popularly known as the DRDA) had a scheme of providing financial assistance to milk co-operatives to develop a portion of public lands as a community managed fodder farm, if the local *panchayat* (local level governance unit) was willing and depending upon its feasibility such as quality of land, availability of water etc. For a drought prone district, with a large population of the cattle herding communities or *Maldharis* as they were locally known (consisting of two sub-communities, i.c. the *Rabaris* and the *Bhurvads*) who depended heavily on livestock as a primary or secondary source of livelihood, combined with deep-rooted traditional beliefs of caring for cattle (and especially the cows), developing a fodder farm that would enable the local families access green fodder throughout the year at reasonable rates was an attractive proposition. Thoriyali was recommended as one of the villages where a good fodder farm could develop as it had the essential pre-requisites – good land, potential water sources and a functioning milk co-operative. AKRSP-I agreed to put in supplementary support in form of bridge financing and technical support and help the co-operative society manage the farm in the initial stages.

Our initial interactions were, as expected, with the village leaders. As a *Rabari* dominated village, the elders were from this community. Among the *Rabaris* too, one particular family was influential. They owned the biggest house, had the most number of cattle, had leased in a stone crushing unit, owned a jeep and a couple of motorcycles and more importantly, wielded political clout. Respected (and possibly feared) by the rest in the village, this family controlled the affairs of the village. But as our visits increased and our contacts grew, the 'second line' became more visible, of course, all men.

This second line was very different from the elders. Aged between 14-24, many of them had at least a few years of schooling, which was significant considering that none of the elders had ever been to school. They had a slightly more 'modern' or 'cosmopolitan' outlook, spoke a smattering of Hindi (the local language was Gujarati which is not very different from Hindi), understood a few words of English, wore trousers and shirts like their urban counterparts (instead of the traditional dress worn by their elders, except on special occasions like weddings and other festivals). Moreover, they seemed to be a little more comfortable with us than the elders were, probably because as youngsters ourselves, we were closer in age to these young men and probably also because in us, they saw some reflection of themselves and their aspirations. They often had lot of questions about our educational and professional background, about what we did to qualify with whatever degrees or diplomas we had and how we were employed by AKRSP-I. They also wanted to know what they should be doing to get a government job (public sector employment was a big thing those days with assurance of a reasonably good pay packet and job security for life, as was the case then and to a large extent, even now).

Of the lot, Alabhai stood out. A young, energetic guy in his mid-twenties, Alabhai was the friendliest and most articulate of the lot. He stood out partly because of his confidence. A guy of an average build and height, he flaunted a stylish (step) haircut. His earrings, which he wore occasionally and his tattooed forearm with Lord Krishna's motif and his own name provided the symbols of tradition to his otherwise 'modern' personality. His smile was bright and revealed a set of perfect teeth and his thick eyebrows knit in concentration while contemplating on what could be done in his village.

Alabhai was a force in his village. At his age, he was the Chairman of the village milk co-operative, which meant that he dealt regularly with the district level dairy officials. His position also brought him in contact with the local block level officials. He often met the local politicians to press for various schemes for his village. More importantly, he seemed to be a role model for the other youth in his village, who looked up to him, took instructions and extended their co-operation to whatever he initiated as a community activity. With equal ease, he related to the village elders, trying to convince them to bury their individual differences or differences between communities for a common cause. His father though was not often happy about his community level work as it meant that he spent much less time for the family business, their farming and managing their cattle. But Alabhai had no qualms. He was confident that his brothers and cousins could help out his father, while he engaged more in community development initiatives.

When the work on the fodder farm started, Alabhai naturally took the lead, as it was under the auspices of the milk co-operative. Initially, there were several meetings. People had to be convinced about allowing a portion of the village commons to be fenced off for a fodder farm. The *panchayat* had to pass the necessary resolutions, which then needed the District Collector's (who was the administrative and revenue head of the district) sanction. After this, the DRDA had to provide a technical sanction and an administrative sanction to ensure that funds under the relevant government programme were released. All this meant that with AKRSP-I, Alabhai had a lot of follow up to do at both the block level (who had to recommend the necessary approvals for their district level officials) and at the district level. It was always an asset to have Alabhai with us. In addition to providing the necessary information, Alabhai had his own way of dealing with the government officials in a firm, assertive manner, but with an enviable degree of diplomacy. He lent a certain credibility to our follow-up meetings as he was a representative from the village and the Chairman of a successful milk co-operative.

Starting the fodder farm provided lot of challenges and opportunities to Alabhai. His administrative skills were put to good use as detailed accounts of money spent and all the supporting documentation had to be systematically maintained. His conflict resolution skills came to the fore as he often took the initiative to resolve several internal conflicts (including some with the neighbouring villages). He also performed an ambassador's role. He often accompanied AKRSP-I staff to other villages where we were not known, addressing community meeting and exhorting them to plan for their village development. His youthfulness and energy infected those in the newer villages who often sought his advice on development opportunities in their respective villages.

At the height of the 1987 drought, with AKRSP-I's support, he led in organising a cattle camp to take care of the village cattle. This meant that in addition to running around for various approvals from the government, he travelled to south Gujarat hunting for good fodder sources. There are quite a few things that I recall about Alabhai and I was always amazed about how much he managed to do, in spite of his youth and the dominance of the elders in the village affairs. But one thing that he did was indeed spectacular, I thought.

This was a village meeting that we were having. He suggested that we could have it in the courtyard of his house that was quite spacious and could accommodate several people. It was a cold, wintry night. People filed in, covering themselves with blankets, huddled and trying to sit as close to the fire that was lit in the middle of the courtyard as possible. Since there was no electricity that day, faces were barely visible. In the dim light there, as people made themselves comfortable, I saw a group of people huddled near the entrance of the courtyard. They were not quite inside, but it was clear that they were not uninterested spectators either. They were here to participate in this meeting. A little while later, as Alabhai noticed them, he said, "Come inside and make yourselves comfortable. If you stand there, you won't be able to participate." A perfectly hospitable gesture, I thought, except that there were some murmurs from a section of the crowd.

Not quite able to fathom the reluctance of those waiting outside, and the rather disconcerted response from a group within, I asked Alabhai what the matter was. "They are *Harijans* (*dalits* or untouchables)", he said plainly, "and as per the general practice in the rural areas, they are not normally allowed inside our homes". I could now understand what the issue was. Alabhai was, in his own way, trying to change the rules of the game. "But I want to change this all. How does it matter that they are *Harijans* ? They are people of this village. There is no problem when they supply milk to the milk co-operative. Why? Because it helps us show better collection figures, and hence, better bonus and profits. So why should anyone mind them coming and participating in a meeting", he asked. Well, perfect logic. But then, a lot of what happens are not generally informed by logic and reason !

I happened to visit Thoriyali several years later, 12 years to be precise, in 2001, while I was on my way to Bhuj which had been badly affected by a powerful earthquake. I had spent a night on AKRSP-I's campus in Sayala from where Thoriyali was just a stone's throw away. As I made my way through the familiar dusty lanes from the main road into Thoriyali, dotted as they were with the '*ganda baval*' (the thorny bush tree that grows in abundance in arid areas, known by its botanical name *prosopis juliflora*) shrubs and littered with cow dung, nothing much seemed to have changed. Some houses looked better, some houses were brightly painted, some lanes were laid with stones, there were more concrete structures, but a look at the people indicated that not much had changed.

As I made my way to meet Alabhai, I was led to a house behind the one that I was used to meeting him in – his father's house.

Alabhai had set up his own home separate from his father's fairly big house. As I entered, he looked at me, partly in disbelief, and partly rather unsure and hesitant of how he should greet me. Alabhai, I was told, and Thoriyali in general was no longer involved with AKRSP-I's programmes after some problems with one of the AKRSP-I supported programmes in the village. That was disappointing though not entirely unanticipated. This was a common recurrence with many villages in the development process when, as programmes develop, NGOs tend to move on to other villages. The older villagers are either 'graduated' or there is a minimal contact with those villages. In some cases, this could also be due to some internal problems, as was the case with Thoriyali.

Alabhai hadn't changed much. The lines on his forehead were deeper and he seemed leaner. He seemed to have lost some of his energy, enthusiasm and natural charm. He seemed more measured, a bit distant too. Strands of grey hair were clearly visible. He eventually warmed up to my unannounced visit. It was clear that much of what had been initiated earlier had not really sustained. The milk co-operative, I was told, was functioning quite well, but the fodder farm had folded up. Alabhai himself had got out of his developmental pursuits in favour of his family business of stone crushing and other bits of civil construction contracting work. In the intermediate, he had also contested local elections but had not succeeded. All this was a bit disappointing as this was one village on which I had lot of hope. But a couple of years later, I realised that all was not, after all, lost.

I was visiting a DFID (UK Government's Department for International Development, where I worked for some time) supported project in western Madhya Pradesh as part of an annual review process in 2003. I was with the Gram Vikas Trust (GVT), an NGO that worked in some parts of Madhya Pradesh, Gujarat and Rajasthan.

Just before one of the sessions was to begin in Ratlam where GVT's team from the three states had assembled, I was told that someone from the Dahod (Gujarat) team wanted to meet me as he knew me. His name was Devsi, they said. The name, though sounding familiar, did not quite ring a bell. As we moved into the meeting room, I looked around for a face that may be familiar, that may belong to Devsi. None. The meeting started. At lunch break, a young man in his mid-twenties came towards me and greeted me. "Do you remember me"? he asked. I didn't and was rather embarrassed. "I am Devsi and I am from Thoriyali", he said. Yes, he now seemed faintly familiar. "I remember the time you used to visit our village very often. I was a teenager then. I used to listen keenly to all the discussions in the meetings. I used to work alongside Haja (a young chap who used to work as the secretary of the milk co-operative) occasionally", he continued.

After completing his intermediate level schooling, he had pursued a Bachelors in Rural Sciences, a course offered by Lok Bharati, an autonomous institute founded by Gandhians in Gujarat's Bhavnagar district. He had then started working with GVT. "We were inspired by the young staff members who came from AKRSP-I. We then realised the value of education and that it was important to take academics seriously. We were constantly goaded by Alabhai to pursue our studies seriously as he felt it was important to do well in academics to be successful in life". Devsi went on. Devsi was from the same community as Alabhai and related to him.

He was excited, narrating all that had happened in his village, that had obviously escaped my notice during my brief visit earlier. And I was delighted to hear all that he had to say. From a time to hardly anyone completing secondary school, Thoriyali could now boast of quite a few graduates and several secondary school pass-outs, many of them girls. Devsi's sister had completed her degree in law. Many other girls, after completing their intermediate school, had plans to pursue their graduation. This was truly a sign of progress.

And Devsi was very clear. "Even if the fodder farm was not successful, I think the fact that we had, through you all, started interacting with the wider world early in our youth, spurred us to look for various options. I am happy to be working here as I can put my knowledge and learning to good use. And moreover, it helps me to work for communities that are not as fortunate as we were in Thoriyali"! he said.

10. The benign Bhima

Bhima – the name evokes images of the Pandava strongman from the Mahabharata, big built, tough and fearless. But this is the story of a Bhima who was, in many ways, quite different.

Bhima was everyone's Man Friday. Bhima was a young man in his early twenties. He belonged to the *Koli Patel* community and hailed from Sapar, a village on the national highway that connected Ahmedabad to Rajkot, in Gujarat.

Bhima was a well built, handsome guy. It was difficult not to notice him. His athletic gait, his broad smile, charming demeanour, his twinkling eyes and his thick moustache were quite conspicuous. A hard working, sincere and honest guy, Bhima was quite popular in the village. He was rumoured to have had affairs with quite a few pretty young lasses, both from his *Koli Patel* community and the *Rabari* community. (That was quite an achievement considering that the more agriculturally inclined *Koli Patels* were always at loggerheads with the *Rabaris* who were cattle herders, with most of the disputes being around the cattle grazing. The *Koli Patels* accused the *Rabaris* of indiscriminate grazing by their cattle and if rumours were to be believed, they deliberately let their cattle into the farms of the *Koli Patels* just as they were getting ready to be harvested !.

I do not remember when and how exactly we befriended Bhima. Probably it was in his *avatar* as a tractor driver. When we started work on renovating the Sapar percolation tank in early 1986 (this was one of the earlier major projects taken up by AKRSP-I, an Ahmedabad-based NGO with whom I worked), we also needed tractors to transport earth that was dug out by those working manually with their spades. Bhima was introduced to us by Devchandbhai, Sapar's respected and shrewd businessman in his sixties, a hard nosed agriculturalist, the local trader, moneylender, a dispute settler, local leader...all rolled into one. The two major communities in the village, the *Koli Patels* and the *Rabaris,* could not ignore Devchandbhai. Not because he was popular, but because he was important and influential.

Bhima was Devchandbhai's trusted lieutenant too. He drove the only tractor in the village that belonged to Devchandbhai. He was a regular on the Devchandbhai's agricultural lands, spread all over the village. He was some sort of a Jack-of-all-trades, and pretty much a good one in almost everything he did. As the tractor driver, he was also a local tractor mechanic. Working on the farms meant that he could repair the diesel motor pump sets. He could tend the crops and knew quite a bit about fertilizers, pesticides and productivity. He could even do odd electrical repair jobs. But Bhima was only partially literate. He had barely gone to school. Hailing from a poor family, Bhima had started working very early in his life and was quite devoted to supporting his family.

He was, in some ways, quite different from the other youth of the area. Unlike his other companions, he never was idle. He was extremely industrious. He did not smoke, drink or while away his time playing cards. Though he did love going to the local block headquarters (Sayala) or the nearest city Rajkot, he rarely indulged himself. He often came back with improved seeds of crops or vegetables, or something useful for his family.

Bhima was a regular on the Sapar tank site for the entire duration of its work during most part of 1986. On days when the tractor was not required, he got down to digging the earth or piling up the stones or any work that was available – and you could always trust him with doing a good job. A quick learner, he was often asked to assist with supervision of the tasks along the 2 kilometres earthen embankment and with his unquestionable integrity, he could be assigned with various responsibilities. This virtue of his was of immense value in the corruption-ridden environment that we were working in, and construction sites was one of the easiest to siphon off money.

One thing that was entirely new for Bhima was community mobilisation, something that AKRSP-I often engaged in. This was something he had never done before. Never before had he been deeply involved with such 'public' responsibilities. The renovation work often meant that there were frequent meetings in the village. Our trusted Bhima would ensure that the message went round and that all were aware of the timings, the venue and even the agenda ! But that was not all. As a deeply sensitive and an intrinsically intelligent person, Bhima had very useful insights to offer. Often he would articulate what others may want to say, but hesitate to do so in a meeting. Bhima had, through this process, discovered something which he was not aware of – his capacity to represent his community and confidence in his ability to articulate their perspectives. Gradually, he started functioning like a secretary of the local association called the *Gram Vikas Mandal*. He even started to learn to read and write (he had some basic literacy skills in spite of not going to school) so that he could take down minutes of village meetings, read out from the muster rolls to mark attendance of people on the sight, and even compute weekly wages.

Bhima set a certain benchmark for us that we kept looking for in village level functionaries in all our project villages with his amazing range of qualities – honest, sincere, hardworking, eager to learn and generally acceptable. That was not easy. When AKRSP-I started exploring working in other villages in the area, we often took Bhima around with us, so that he could talk about what had happened in his village and so that the village youth could find someone to connect with, a role model, someone who understood their environs, their culture and more importantly, their perspectives and aspirations.

As our work in Sapar came to an end, our interaction with the village and Bhima reduced. We had more villages to work in, there were more concerns, more projects. But we did make it a point to seek him out whenever we visited Sapar or passed through – and invariably, he would be busy either with his own work or with helping others. Bhima must be in fifties now. He must have got married. He probably has children. His ex-girlfriends probably still yearn for him. He has probably joined politics and contested local elections. He is probably a very successful farmer and entrepreneur. And he certainly would continue to be an asset to his village and his people, someone that the younger generation can look forward to for inspiration and emulation.

11. Samuben sows an idea !

It was in early 1986 that AKRSP-I started working on renovating the Sapar percolation tank (for conserving rainwater) in Surendranagar district of Gujarat. I had joined this team towards the end of 1985. Surendranagar was an arid area and often suffered from drought. Agriculture was certainly not an assured source of income. In fact, more often than not, people depended on the state government sponsored drought relief works for employment. Working conditions used to be terrible, payments irregular, corruption rampant and worse, such works caused disputes within the village, among families, between people of different caste or social group. If nothing worked, migration to the far off southern districts of Gujarat was the only way   out.

AKRSP-I had initiated this work in consultation with the local community. 'Participation' was still a new concept and certainly on government funded works which were 'technical' in nature. We had got commitment for most of the funds from the state government and had agreed to put in some resources of our own. However, it was clear from the beginning and especially to the government, that AKRSP-I would do this work using its own methodologies, and hence, in many   ways,   would   be   'different'.

It was with great curiosity and a great deal of amusement that the women heard from their male counterparts that the AKRSP-I team wanted them too to be in the meeting. "How could they come for these meetings"? the men wondered. "They have work at home, they need to cook and take care of the children. How would they find time to come for meetings"? one of the men asked. "Even if they come, they won't be able to say anything, as their men folk would be there. Most

47

of them would be their relatives and elders of the village and hence would observe the *'laaj'* (meaning, would cover their faces). It is meaningless and rather uncalled for", said one of the elders who couldn't understand this fuss being made about meeting and involving women! "Why don't you tell us when the work will start and how much will you pay and how many people you want on the worksite"? asked one of the younger men. "We will ensure that there is adequate number of people to do your   work".

It took a great deal of Anilbhai's (the first Chief Executive of AKRSP-I and a retired officer from the Gujarat cadre of the Indian Administrative Service) patience and persuasion to explain that this was a different work and it was 'their' work. It was something on which they had to develop a stake, take pride in and ensure technical excellence. This was for a long term good as renovating the reservoir would mean plenty of water for the village, for irrigation, for the cattle for several years to come. It would mean recharging of wells and better productivity. It would mean women wouldn't have to trudge long distances to fetch water or fuel or fodder. And more importantly, since women's stakes were also involved, it was important that women also took part in all the decisions being made on this work.

The women too were admittedly baffled. Never had anyone sought their opinion even on matters concerning themselves or their own families. No one asked them if they were ready for marriage. No one asked if they wanted to bear children. No one asked them if they wanted to go to school. No one asked them if they were being paid wages for their labour. No one asked if they had their meal. No one asked if they need to take a break from long hours of working. No one just about asked them anything. Just because, they were only meant to do what was expected of them - no questions asked ! Oh well, they did ask them if the food was ready. Their husbands and sons did ask them for that extra bit of cash. They did ask them if they had milked the cows and sold the milk. But that was it.

"What value can we add to these discussions", they asked innocently. "After all, our men folk know everything that needs to be done. And moreover, we have so much of work to do at home"! "With the older men sitting in these meetings, how do you expect us to talk", one of the younger women asked. "We will be observing 'laaj' or else we will be severely reprimanded by our in-laws and others in the village". It certainly did not help us that we did not have any woman on our team. (Till a few months later, when Sonal joined, by which time the work on the Sapar reservoir had started, we didn't have any woman on our team. Seeing Sonal as part of our team seemed to boost the confidence of the women, who then seemed to be more relaxed in our presence).

When the work started, it was clear to the people that they would earn more in wages than what they would otherwise have earned, had this been done through a contractor or even directly by the government department. Moreover the process would be very transparent. Anilbhai was therefore keen that a part of the wages, roughly amounting to 10% was set aside as savings. This idea certainly did not appeal to the men. They did not trust the intentions of 10% of their wages being withheld as they had several terrible experiences in the past of being cheated of their wages.The women, though not very sure, seemed to be willing to consider.

Over a period of time, it was clear that the 10% did not really pinch, especially since it was being set aside for some use in future and our regular presence had started building some trust. They were happy that in a drought year, they were earning decent wages even excluding the 10% compulsory savings, which was much higher than what they had ever earned before with the unscrupulous contractors siphoning off huge amounts from their earnings, or straightaway refusing to pay them for their work ! The working conditions were something that they had probably never experienced before. There was a place for people to relax during the hot summer afternoons, regular supply of clean drinking water, and more importantly for the women, an 'ayah' to take care of their children – an onsite crèche, which was absolutely unheard of.

Not that Bharatbhai, our engineer supervising the work was happy about. On secondment from the state government, he often wondered why AKRSP-I was hell bent on breaking the norms and spoiling the 'labourers' ! The extreme weather conditions which made him dash every now and then to gulp down a pitcher of cool water was not reason enough for him to consider that those working in the hot merciless summer straining every single muscle of their body may also need a relief. "They are resilient, and are just used to working in these conditions", was his constant refrain, much to my colleague, Shashi's annoyance !

The hectic pace of work during the hot summer months which involved over 500 people saw the work completed by the first week of June 1986, just in time for receiving the fresh monsoon waters. There was an animated expectation among the villagers to see their reservoir fill with water, the first time in several years, which, they knew, would last till the next monsoon. In fact, most people in the village had not seen the reservoir even partially full. Built under state government's drought relief programme to poor technical specifications and implemented by corrupt but influential contractors whom the government officials dared not confront or challenge, each time the reservoir was renovated, it would last only till the following monsoon season before being breached at several places, thus rendering it utterly useless. With the monsoon now approaching and a change in the air we detected, we decided to have a meeting to discuss how we could use the money saved, which, by then, had amounted to thousands of rupees.

"Distribute it equally among us. We will use it for something, maybe we will buy something", said Nanjibhai. Most of the men seemed to nod in agreement. The women however did not seem convinced. There was a murmur among them but when asked, they just laughed. The discussion kept moving along the lines of 'distribute it equally'. And we kept on asking them to consider better options.

Sonal moved closer to the women, encouraging them too to think of options. One of the women said "As the men say, distribute the money among us and we will buy utensils". The other women laughed again. They were quite amused at the idea of getting all the cash to get those beautiful brass and steel vessels they always wanted! But the men weren't amused. "What a waste", one of them said. That was enough to shut the women. But Sonal persisted.

Rather hesitantly, Samuben, one of the most active women on the worksite stood up. She said, "Get us seeds with that money", she said, hesitantly. There was a sudden quiet among the crowd. She looked around, unsure of what the reaction of the others would be, rather diffidently. But one could see the resolve on her face. Turning back to us, she said in a slightly more confident tone, "Yes, give us seeds". She continued, "You see, it is the sowing season now, but most of us do not have seeds. As soon as the first rains come, our men will run around for seeds, but we wouldn't have enough money. They will then buy seeds on credit from the local traders, which invariably will not be of good quality, as all the good quality seeds would have been bought by the richer farmers prior to the arrival of the rains. We end up getting poor quality seeds at high rates of interest, and that also, late. How can you expect us to reap a good harvest"?

We heard her speak, in amazement. This was a very sensible and relevant suggestion. Anilbhai, listening with rapt attention to what Samuben had to say, smiled. He was delighted. What a productive way on using this money! Samuben had just explained an economic reality so simply, which, if addressed effectively, would provide a very sustainable source of livelihood, year after year. He looked at us and said, "Did you hear what she said? It is very significant. Note it down", which we promptly   did!

He then turned to her and said, "Samuben, you have made an extremely good suggestion". Samuben blushed. Suddenly, all eyes were trained on her. She was even embarrassed. Pulling her saree over her head consciously and partly covering her face, she sat down hurriedly, wanting to escape from the peering eyes. There was a smile on her face. That one moment of attention meant like a lifetime achievement for her. But she was also apprehensive. Did she say something wrong? Forget the others, but will her husband reprimand her? She darted a glance at Popatbhai, her husband. Popatbhai was smiling. And why not ? The thought of enough money for seeds at the time of rains was something that they could possibly never have dreamed about. We could trace a shade of pride in Popatbhai's smile. After all, it was his wife's idea and for once, it seemed he was content for his wife to grab the limelight.

Anilbhai turned back to those assembled and said, "I have an additional suggestion. We will organize to buy the seeds jointly. We will get good quality seeds from

Gandhinagar (the capital of Gujarat state), from the State Seeds Corporation. These will be certified seeds which will yield a good harvest". Everyone nodded in agreement. Samuben's suggestion had gone down well and so had Anilbhai's.

"But", Anilbhai continued, "you will have to pay back the cost of seeds after the harvest, he said. The group was surprised. Why should they pay back for something which was bought with their own money? "As Samuben said, you need seeds year after year, season after season. If you repay the cost of seeds, we will buy more seeds for the next season. That way, you will have a fund which will be replenished with your own money. Once you are comfortable with the idea, you may even want to charge a nominal interest, so that your fund grows to meet your growing needs. And your money will remain in your own village".

This seemed to be an interesting suggestion, but not a very convincing one. (Mind you, this was at a time when micro-credit or micro-finance had not yet become popular, nor had the concept of self-help groups emerged). The crowd was quiet. Samuben got up again and this time, with a greater degree of confidence, she said, "Anilbhai, you are very right. We need money for seeds every season, every year. We must create this fund with repayments for the cost of seeds. However, if some people don't refund, they will not be eligible for this scheme the following season".

Slowly, there seemed to be a consensus emerging. Little did Anilbhai or we realize that the seeds of a savings and credit scheme which would grow into several millions of rupees over the years across hundreds of villages, had been sown. Samuben had sown the seed of an idea which was a small revolution for AKRSP-I, but a huge step forward for the hundreds of families we worked with!

12. The children of Kallupatti

It was September 1988. Ajit Mani and I were on our way from Bangalore to Madurai to G. Kallupatti, a village of Madurai district, where Reaching the Unreached (RTU) was based. "This place is full of children", Ajit had mentioned. An organisation supported by ActionAid, I was being considered for being seconded to RTU to assist Bro. Kimpton. Ajit was then the Field Director for South India with ActionAid. "And if you like children, you will fall in love with RTU, and of course, you will be in the good books of Brother James Kimpton", he said.

Bro. Kimpton was a British missionary of the De La Salle order, who had been working in Madurai since the sixties, setting up homes for children, schools for poor children and vocational training centres, having worked for a couple of decades before in Sri Lanka (or Ceylon, then). It was pretty quiet when we reached Kallupatti, late in the evening, not a bit like what Ajit was preparing me for. "Don't get deceived" cautioned Ajit. "They will all be here peering through the windows in the morning". He was referring to the children, most of them orphaned and destitute who lived in neatly built small one-bedroom cottages, being cared for by a woman who was a 'foster' mother for the children. And true enough, they were all there when I went to the veranda to have my morning tea.

Initially, they were a bit shy – girls and boys of varying ages. But they all had a bright, welcoming smile. And in a matter of minutes, they had managed to perch themselves at the edge of the veranda, probably realising that we were harmless. "*Mama, unga paer enna*" (uncle, what is your name ?), they asked in Tamil, trying to become more familiar. That innocuous question and the answer to it literally lifted the sluice valve for questions to flow in. They were no more in ones and twos. The questions were in chorus. And in Tamil, a language I barely understood then. Obviously, the answer to most of the questions was a smile, a smile and more smiles !

That was the beginning of my orientation to the famed children of RTU. There was the day care centre, the *balwadis* (pre-primary centres), the full time primary schools, the supplementary schools (for those studying in the poorly managed local government schools), the vocational training centres, the foster homes. In all, about 2000 children with whom RTU directly worked with, not to mention the thousands of children the RTU team was regularly in contact with through their other programmes !

It was mandatory for Bro. Kimpton to take an afternoon walk through the village. Pied Piper like, he would be followed by umpteen children greeted with lusty shouts of *"Thatha, vanakkam"* (greetings, grandfather) all along. Yes, he was popularly known as 'Thatha' or 'grandfather', even by the adults (much to his annoyance at times!). He was a familiar sight, yet the children would reach out to him, to hold his hand, invite him to their houses for a cup of tea. Often, in the evenings, Bro. Kimpton would sit outside his little office room to greet the children as they went back home from school and he would indulge them with boiled candies (or *mittai*, as the children referred to. *'Thatha, mittai'*....was their constant demand).

When I eventually joined RTU in early 1989, I had an office room right next to Bro. Kimpton's. It was always a delight to see the children walk by, run by, shout along as they made their way to their school or home, often peeping through my window to check what I was doing, sometimes, coming in up to my desk for a quick chat. Holidays in schools and vacations were truly boring times on the campus (remember that popular Tamil film song *'April – May-elay, pasumay yen illae, kaanj poch da'*.......why is there no greenery in April and May, everything looks so dry ?). Though that song was sung in a different context by a bunch of boys in college, ruing about the absence of girls on college campuses in the summer vacation, I found myself humming that song in April and May, when children were a rare sight on the RTU campus.

13. Bro. Kimpton's foster children

Foster children were very special and dear to Bro. Kimpton and RTU's staff. They came from very difficult backgrounds and I often wondered how these children could still be so cheerful and determined after going through so much so early in their lives. Most of them were girls, some of them having been rescued from being killed by their own parents as they did not want daughters. Some were dumped because they were illegitimate. Some were orphaned because one or both their parents were dead, some in violent situations that they were unfortunately witness to. Some were severely disabled. But one thing that each one of them found in great abundance at RTU was love and care. They all were welcome. No child in need was turned away. The children too had an amazing way of welcoming a new child in their midst and making them comfortable in their new environs. I got to know some of these children very well and was always struck by how they managed to overcome their adversities. I wish to write about some of them. (Names of these children have been changed).

One of the first children I got to know and made friends with was Belinda, who was then less than 10. Ajit used to support her education and was particularly fond of her. A bright smile, a warm greeting and the spirit to overcome her physical disability was what one remembers of her very vividly. She was one of the 120 foster children being cared for by RTU.

Then there were the two sisters – Priya and Preeti, both very bright, pretty and naughty, very unlike the other girls on the campus. One could hardly imagine that their father would have ever even thought of abandoning his wife and two vivacious daughters to get married to another woman.

The more unfortunate case was that of Jaya. Her father had deserted her mother soon after she was born, in spite of promising her repeatedly to marry her. Being an illegitimate child meant overcoming several adversities. Her mother, meanwhile, had fallen in love with a decently employed young man, who agreed to marry her if she got 'rid' of her child. Wanting her daughter to grow in a safe environment, Jaya was brought to Kallupatti. She rarely saw her mother. You could see it in her eyes – the longing for her 'own' mother, though of course, she was well taken care of in her adopted home. She bloomed there, good in studies and excelling in dancing. Her handwork was exquisite, her cooking fantastic.

Nandini did not know where she came from. She was cared for Valliammal for many years, till her foster mother grew too old to care for her. She then moved with a family who legally adopted her. She excelled academically. She was an excellent, expressive dancer. Her lisp was endearing and so was her smile. It's difficult to imagine now, but she is now a qualified medical doctor. She is very clear that she would like to give back to society something of what she got from it – caring. She plans to work with a local NGO and provide health care to the poor.

The boys, as I said, were fewer, but were quite a visible, voluble lot. There was Peter and Thomas, two brothers, aged 10 and 7 when I first met them. Both were dark skinned, had bright eyes shining with mischief, and always wore a dazzling smile, blinding enough to hide the pain they had undergone of seeing their mother being killed by their father in a fit of rage. Their father was serving a prison sentence.

And there was Vishwa, quiet and mature, unlike most boys of his age. He had been abandoned by his parents for unknown reasons. Short and round faced, he was extremely bright, fared well academically, was his teachers' favourite and wanted to grow up to be a doctor. His academic achievements set benchmarks for the other children and he was generally popular, except with his foster-brothers whose rather poor academic performance was often compared with Vishwa's.

14. The boys' hostel

One of the challenges for me, but also a delightful task, was of managing a boys' hostel right next to my house. Though not very keen on discipline myself, I had to ensure a semblance of discipline among a bunch of boisterous boys, 15 of them, in the age group of 6 to 16 ! Most were either orphans or had lost a parent. All were from very poor families who stay and schooling was being supported. (Names of the children have been changed).

There was the rebel, Palanivel, one of the older guys. A tough and muscular guy, he was a bully, deft with his fingers, rather adventurous, trouble maker at times, but always willing to put in as much physical labour as one would want. The guy had stamina. Thangaraj was a complete contrast. Tall and frail, oldest among the lot, he was mature, responsible, cared for the younger boys and was keen to take on teaching as a career. Muthu, whose father had abandoned his mother and the children, was an eternal cynic, partly from his background and partly because of his chronic asthma. His poor health meant that he always carried around medicines with him. Most of it was self medication though. He was an artist. The only thing that interested him was painting and crafts. He was nicknamed 'Medicine' by the boys because of the amount of medicines he took. He was lazy to the core and just didn't care about anyone or anything.

Karthikeyan, Joseph and Raman, all about 13, vied for my and Sandhya's (my wife) attention, wanting to be allotted small errands to be in our good books, so that they could get away with a little bit of bullying the younger children and a little bit of defying the hostel rules! Then there was Arunan, who was about 14. Strong and wiry like Palanivel, but quiet and responsible like Thangaraj. He was not into studies, but was a sincere student, keen to pursue vocational skills and support his family. The quietest of the lot though was 13-year old

Sakthivel. Abandoned by his step mother after the death of his father and also by his own elder brother after he got married, Sakthivel had a severe physical handicap because of which he could not walk properly. The other kids called him 'Dancer', rather unkindly, but he never bothered about that. He had overcome several more adversities in his short life and he would just smile genially !

The youngest among them was Karthik and Murali, delightful 6 year olds who always fought with each other, would weep each time their mothers came to meet them and returned, would invariably get bullied by the older boys, have their special ration of boiled eggs snatched away, but were generally popular. Murali did not last there for long. After staying on for a year, he made two unsuccessful attempts to run away, but was always brought back. After his third attempt, he never returned. I think he had a rather interesting summer break when he made friends with some boys back home. We were told that he spent the entire summer vacation wandering with the other boys, bathing in the village pond, doing odd errands and making small money, which they then spent on movies in the local theatre. For some reason, he missed them terribly and his heart was not in the hostel. We missed him too.

Some of them are doing very well. Thangaraj had started working with RTU as a teacher, even while I was with RTU in 1993, after having completed his diploma and while continuing to pursue more academic pursuits. Meanwhile, he also organised his sister's wedding including finding her a suitable groom, whom he also supported with a vocational training course. Karthikeyan works in Tiruppur in one of the hosiery units. He once telephoned me, almost five years after I had last seen him in 1993. He said he was earning Rs. 4,000 a month and that he was also taking care of his widowed mother and his younger brother, who lived with him. He was keen that his younger brother got a proper education. I knew Karthikeyan had a good heart, even if he was a bully and a rather smooth operator, who was smart at breaking the hostel rules ! Arunan must have completed his polytechnic diploma course. I used to meet him once a month when he came to our office to collect his monthly scholarship we had offered him for his course. He seemed to be doing well and I hope he is well employed now.

Karthik and Raman are in some odd occupations. I believe Raman is working in the same stationery shop in Madurai where his father worked. Well, he used to work there even in the summer vacations when he went back to his father, partly because his step mother didn't want him around the house. I am not sure if he was able to continue with his studies. Karthik was a bright, lively kid, though he never did well in studies. I had hoped he would join some vocational training course on the campus, but then, he too left the campus to live with his widowed mother in Madurai for reasons I am not clear about. I heard that he was working in a cycle repair shop, something that I was not happy about. He could have done much better.

I have no news of Palanivel, except that he had fallen in love with a girl from his village and eventually got married to her. Muthu is married now and has a daughter. Sakthivel unfortunately committed suicide while in his early twenties due to huge debts that he had incurred, leading a directionless life, once he quit the hostel. It was also partly due to depression because his brother, the only relative with whom he had some contact, disowned him over a family dispute !

Being in close contact with these boys who came from very deprived backgrounds was indeed an unforgettable experience. Each one had a story to tell, often an unhappy one, which they often tried to forget while they were together, engaging in the daily routine of their studies, playing, keeping the hostel clean and a bit of gardening. A visit from one of their relatives, or a visit home would bring them back to the 'real' world that they eventually had to live in. Often I would see one of the children sitting in a dark, unlit corner of the veranda, reminiscing about something that he held dear, or worrying about something that they were not keen to share. Once in a while, they would come and talk to me, just to unburden and not looking for solutions. I am not in touch with any of them. Looking back, I just hope that the life in the hostel provided them with an environment that made them stronger, more determined to face the challenges of life, and prepare them for meeting these head on. What else could an institution do ?

15. Gender based discrimination – as perceived by children

Children have an amazing sense of articulation, which is not often understood or recognised. And it has nothing to do with their educational background.

Anita, a friend and colleague of mine during my days with Plan International, was discussing the issue of gender discrimination with a group of men and women, boys and girls separately. This was sometime in the late 1990s. This was in Dharmapuri district of Tamil Nadu, where the practice of female infanticide was common (as also in Salem and Madurai districts). Anita was trying to understand the perspective of the local community on the why, what and how of discrimination against girl children. She met initially with a group of men and women. The men stoutly denied any form of discrimination against girls. They fed them well, treated them well, provided them with all the opportunities that they would provide a girl child, they said. The women were defensive and even rationalised the forms of discrimination. Ultimately she has to go to another house, so why educate her more? It will be difficult to find a match later. Moreover, as a woman, she must learn to give priority to her husband's needs and hence, must eat last, even eat less if there isn't enough, they said.

The girls however refuted and contested what their mothers said. "We are strongly being discriminated against", they said. "Our brothers get more clothes. They always get a priority in case of education. Many of us are not allowed to continue due to economic reasons or on reaching puberty. But the boys have no such hassles. Even if they are not interested in studies and don't do well, they continue to be sent to school. They hardly do any work at home. We have to take care of our younger siblings too if our mothers are busy", they narrated.

We expected this view to be contested by the boys who may even justify the preferential treatment they got. But we were in for a surprise. "We know the girls get a raw deal", they said. "They eat less, get fewer clothes, do not enjoy the leisure that we have. We know it is wrong, very wrong. But we don't know what to do about it. If we try to do some work that the girls are supposed to like cleaning the house or fetching water or washing our clothes or cooking, our parents scold us and friends deride us. They ask us why are we doing stuff that only girls are meant to do ? And ultimately, we get to do only what our adults want us to do, isn't it? How do you expect us to change the existing situation if the adults don't want us to change"?

There was a similar response, this time from the girls. I was travelling through Chengalpettu district in Tamil Nadu. Most men and boys were huddled around the lone black and white TV set, watching a day and night India – Zimbabwe one day cricket match. So engrossed were they that they barely turned their heads around to see us alighting from a jeep, something which is rather uncommon. "Good relief", we thought, as otherwise, our interactions with village communities are normally dominated by the men, barely allowing their women to have a word through, unless, of course when asked to shut up !

The women and the girls were busy with their household chores – cooking dinner, milking the cow, washing utensils, bringing back head loads of dry fuel wood. Out of curiosity, I asked some of the girls, "Wouldn't you also like to see the cricket match"? The girls broke out into helpless giggles as if I had said something ridiculous. "How can they watch TV? Why should they ? They don't understand the bat and ball game", said one of the women. "Why? Why not"? I asked. "Oh, they don't understand and they are not interested. Moreover, who will help us cook our dinner and attend to other household chores"? they queried.

But this time, it was the girls who responded. "We want to watch the TV and we want to see cricket. If we don't get to see, how will we know what this game of cricket is all about? But we can't. Our elders....our mothers say we can't. You see, if we don't help them, the household work won't get done and our fathers will get very angry. The boys always get away by doing nothing. They while away their time, watch TV, pick up fights, yet no one admonishes them", they said. No, they were not complaining and there was no bitterness in their voices. They were just narrating to us a reality they faced and a discrimination that they experienced, day in and day out, being denied the privileges that their brothers could avail and they could not, for no fault of theirs – just because they were girls and this is how they were destined to live ! Which incidentally they had come to accept, with a great degree of bitterness though.....and will probably perpetrate, unknowingly, when they grow up and become mothers too! This was social conditioning in action.

Similar stories and incidents kept surfacing in several parts of the country I visited. In one village in Karnataka, girls stopped going to school because they were constantly teased, not just by the older boys, but even some adults from their own communities. "Do you think you are going to become a District Collector", they would ask derisively, followed by loud guffaws. But this was only the mildest form of harassment. Many girls had worse forms of harassment to narrate, abused by older boys in their schools, and sometimes, even by their male teachers!

In a village in Betul district of Madhya Pradesh, girls were stopped from continuing their studies beyond standard 5 as their parents thought it would be difficult then to get a suitable groom for them. Children in a small Orissa village in Kashipur district of Orissa preferred not to go to school, a few kilometres away, fearing wild animals. And the adults did not consider it worthwhile to escort these children, especially if they were girls – for what use was education to a girl child in a small tribal village in Orissa?

The situation in the relatively more developed Tamil Nadu, and that too, in Chennai, was equally distressing. In a high school in Chennai, right in the backyard of its famed film industry, girl children stopped going to school just because there were no toilets, something which they found it difficult to manage without, especially on attaining puberty. It was in a government girls' school named after a Marwari businessman who had donated some money for the school to be named after him. For relieving themselves, the girls had to use a stretch of land right next to the railway track, a little distance from their school – which obviously they found it difficult with the frequency of trains passing by.

It was amidst such dismal adversities that we met Lakshmi in a small remote village of Chamrajnagar district in Karnataka. We were in a village on a dark, rainy day, well past 8 p.m. with no electricity supply in the entire village. Her own house did not have an electricity connection, but the streetlight was always helpful. As the only child of her parents, her parents had given top priority to educating her. Her parents' determination to see through her education was indeed remarkable, not commonly seen. She had to walk to the middle school, 6 kilometres away. Each day, she walked for more than an hour to go to school and an hour to get back. There were only 3 children including Lakshmi who went to the middle school, mainly because of the distance. All the others had dropped out. 2 were boys. Lakshmi, the only girl, normally found herself walking alone since the boys were not too keen on escorting her. But these difficulties did not bother Lakshmi. She was determined to be educated, qualify as a teacher, and come back to teach children in her village.

16. Overcoming disabilities

That was the same determination I saw in Husaina Banu. Daughter of a prominent local Muslim trader Shahbuddin, she was afflicted by polio at a very young age. She was almost immobile. Several sessions in the local physiotherapy centre of RTU which her father ensured she never missed, had ensured that she could at least start walking slowly and with difficulty, with the help of callipers and crutches. It was indeed a heart warming sight. In an area notorious for female infanticide where it was also not uncommon for girl children to be abandoned or ignored, Husaina Banu's father was truly inspiring, thanks to whose motivation, many other children with physical disability were also brought out of their homes, the charming Selvi being one of them. One should have seen the delight on her face when, slowly, but surely, she took her first steps, on her own, with a pair of crutches and callipers, almost 6 years after she was born!

Over a period of time, I saw Husaina and Selvi also carrying their own school bags, politely refusing help from their schoolmates, confident that they had overcome a major hurdle in their lives. Husaina excelled in studies, Selvi in drawing and artwork. Husaina was a good singer too. Her mellifluous voice wafted through the morning school assemblies. Invariably, she led the other children in reciting the morning prayers in school. Shahbuddin's pride in the recognition that his daughter had gained, was perceptible as he would lean against one of the school pillars, beaming, to hear his daughter beautiful voice over the school's public address system. And Selvi's father Murugan never stopped smiling each time he saw Selvi making her way to school, on her own, confident that she could be quite independent.

And then, there was Saravanan. How could one ever forget him ? He was about 7 when I first met him in 1989 during my time with RTU. Hailing from a poor *dalit* family, I had got used to his peeping through my office window in the morning while he was on his way to school. His bright eyes and his toothy smile lit up his dark, handsome face as he would shout out a 'Good morning *saaaar* (sir)' ! to me each morning. Saravanan, like Husaina Banu and Selvi, was a regular at the physiotherapy centre. Dutifully, he would arrive in the morning, on his father's old bicycle. For those who worked in the unit too, it was a routine for them to be greeted by his loud 'Good morning *akka* (older sister in Tamil)' and 'Good morning *anney* (older brother in Tamil)' greetings, after which he would get down to his exercises and the oil massages. His was a very serious case of locomotor disability. At home, he would be moving, crawling about, on all fours. No disability could ever dent his enthusiasm for mischief though!

One day, he was taken to a nearby hospital, where a generous orthopaedic surgeon, Dr. Karuppaiah, known for his philanthropy, performed a crucial hip operation. It took several weeks of recuperation. One fine day, it was Saravanan's D-day. For the first time in his life, he would not be carried to school by his father, as was normally the case.

He allowed his father to bring him on his old bicycle only till the campus gate. Gingerly, he got off the bicycle with his father's help and started walking – his first steps ever since he was born. His hips, fresh from the operation, ached, and he grimaced. The callipers felt as if it weighed a ton, but Saravanan's determination was clearly visible on this face. It seemed he needed all his strength to move the crutches, first the right, then the left – all of which yielded the one result he wanted....the step forward, the first one, on his own! He grimaced again, but you could not miss the grit and determination on his face. He waved cheerfully at those in the physiotherapy unit which was nearest to the campus gate with whom he was very popular and who were just amazed to see him walk, and perhaps quite emotional too. It was a good 200 meters' walk to his school, straight down from the campus gate. His father had ensured that they come in early enough so that Saravanan could tread this long distance to be in time for the morning assembly.

As he passed the office blocks, the handloom weaving unit, the batik unit on his way to the school, all work seemed to come to a standstill. All eyes were on Saravanan, popular as he was, but more than that, for them to witness a big day in his life......for everyone wanted to witness that great moment in Saravanan's life. Finally, he was almost there. A final right turn near a hand pump on the campus would take him to the school grounds where the children would have assembled for their morning prayers. It had taken him almost half-an-hour for him to cover the distance of a mere 200 meters - a monumental effort indeed, with just an occasional support from his father, who accompanied him, happiness and pride very visible on his face as he witnessed his son walking......for the first time ever in this life!

It was quiet on the ground where about 250 children had assembled solemnly for their prayers, unaware of this great moment in Saravanan's life. Suddenly, a group of children who formed the rear rows of the assembly, sighted Saravanan inching towards them, with his father right behind, holding his school bag. "Hey, look here! Saravanan has started walking", one of them shouted excitedly, even while the teachers were trying to quieten the assembly for the morning prayers. Heads turned. Saravanan's smile widened to see his school mates, who were undoubtedly astonished! And it happened all of a sudden ....they broke into an impromptu applause. It was like a standing ovation. Children and teachers, and some parents who had escorted their children to school applauded. It was a mixture of joy, surprise and relief., and lots of emotions By now, Saravanan was tired. His legs were giving way. His hands were stiff. But the sudden applause seemed to rejuvenate him. He looked up, proud and happy. His smile widened, his dark face brightened. He knew he had achieved something. There were many moist eyes....... !

Saravanan's determination, and that of Husaina Banu and Selvi, did not go unnoticed. The children of their school were witness to these determined children overcoming their physical disabilities and seemed, in a way, to send out a clear message. The children too were empathetic. They were there to help when required, but in a very unobtrusive and non-patronising way and in complete solidarity.

Sita (name changed) was different. What struck one about her was her cheerfulness and her big bright eyes. But she was different. She was abandoned and found in a bus stop by some villagers because of her severe disability. Her head was disproportionately large. She did not seem to have much control over her body, and especially the limbs - clearly, it would have been very difficult for her to walk even when she grew up. Her speech was incoherent and her gaze unsteady. But she had a sharp mind. Initially, there was some concern about how she could be taken care of and if any of the foster mothers would be able to take care of. That's when Parvati, one of the foster mothers, volunteered to be Sita's foster mother. She was confident she could provide all the love and care that was required to develop Sita's capabilities.

Sita started visiting the physiotherapy centre for her exercises and massage that could strengthen her limbs. She was only two then. Gradually, as she became more comfortable in her new surroundings, and as she picked up new words, she became talkative. Initially, it sounded like meaningless chatter as the words got twisted as she started speaking. Slowly, it became clearer. She started recognising people by name. She would shout out aloud to Ramesh as he did the rounds of the foster homes for regular maintenance work. Ramesh *mama* (uncle) was her favourite *mama*. He always had time for her - for Ramesh, Sita was very special ! She would climb on his back, ruffle his hair, put both her arms lovingly around him and keep pleading with him not to go. I made it a point to visit her as frequently as possible, largely because I loved meeting her and listening to her latest chatter, and partly to escape being admonished by her. "You did not come to see me", she would say if she didn't see me for a couple of days.

I met Sita after a gap of five years, in 1998. "Do you know me"? I asked. She came close to me. I did seem familiar to her. She put her hand on my shoulder, kept gazing at me for a few minutes. She then looked at my wife. And then back to me. "Girish *mama* !", she exclaimed, "and Sandhya *aththai* (aunty)" ! She was delighted. And then she started talking, excitedly as ever. "Where were you? Why didn't you come to see me? I am going to school now........." I was not surprised that I felt a lump in my throat ! We always knew she was sharp .... and smart ....and special !

17. Superman's 'mess' !

We all called in 'Subramani's Mess'. No, it was not a mess he created. It was what the staff canteen was known as, a rather colloquial expression - the place where you got the most delicious food made with loving care by Subramani.

He was about 15 when he came to RTU, sometime in 1986. He was an orphan. His mother was his father's second wife. They lived near Kodaikanal, in the hills. They barely eked out a living from a small plot of land which they cultivated. When Subramani's father died, his elder step brother, who was then in his early twenties, drove away Subramani and his mother. He was barely a couple of years old – or so he believes. His mother came down to Vathalagundu, a small town on the foothills of the Kodai hills and took up odd jobs to keep themselves alive. There, she befriended a Muslim family, who helped her from time to time when she did not find work. Eventually, they became very attached to the family.

When Subramani was just about four, his mother too died, possibly, of tuberculosis. Years passed by. While the kind Muslim family fed him, Subramani took up small jobs, sometimes in a shop, sometimes in a restaurant. One fine day, someone who claimed to be his uncle, came from Kodaikanal, looking for him. He took Subramani with him, who went along happily on finding someone from his own family.

But his delight was short lived. The so-called uncle did not send Subramani to school as promised. Instead, he asked Subramani to work on his farm, tend his cattle and generally, provide cheap labour. All he got in return was some measly food, and that too very inadequate, and a place to sleep.

One day, he decided enough was enough. He got on to a truck that was coming down to Vathalagundu, paying Rs. 2 to the driver. That was all the money he had. He had heard of a village for orphaned boys from someone who came to visit his so-called uncle. He didn't find the orphanage. Instead, he landed up, tired, hungry and malnourished, at the Leonard Hospital a hospital run by the sisters of the Presentation Convent (a Catholic order of missionaries), who in turn, asked him to meet Bro. Kimpton in Kallupatti, 10 kms away. He spent the night on the veranda of the hospital. Fortunately, the sisters of the convent there fed him a simple meal.

The next day, early in the morning, he reached Kallupatti. The medical clinic had not yet opened. He was the first to reach there. Tired as he was and nervous, he lay on one of the benches in front of the clinic. He could barely sit up. The long hours of work, the travel, the hunger and the mental stress had all taken a toll on him. He looked pale and was very weak Soon, the medical clinic staff came and on hearing his story, he was taken to meet Bro. Kimpton. "Feed him first, get him a decent set of clothes and then we will see", Bro. Kimpton instructed.

Since he was about 15 then, he was too old for the foster homes. He seemed too old for the boys' hostel too and moreover, he was a non-school going child. But then that's where Bro. Kimpton decided to put him. Meanwhile, Sister Sandra who supervised the clinic, took a personal interest in nursing him back, treating him like her own brother. Since Subramani could not go to school, he spent most of his time in the clinic. In a short period, he had befriended the clinic staff and even some of the regular patients. He was always there to help around with various errands – making paper envelopes for medicines, bandages for the poor patients, serving meals to the old aged in their homes, cleaning the clinic after working hours and even taking care of the plants which Sister Sandra had fondly planted behind the clinic.

Almost a year passed. Subramani regained his health and became a popular person around - with his infectiously dazzling smile and positive attitude. It was at that time that a need for an assistant cook was felt since there were more staff using the staff 'mess'. Subramani was delighted when he was asked if he could assist the cook in the mess, because it meant learning new skills (he was always interested in cooking) and also a princely salary of Rs. 150 with free food ! As a teenager, he was a quick learner and a very hard worker. He scrubbed the vessels, cleaned the floors and set the meal in the mess. Initially, he started with less important tasks like cutting and cleaning vegetables. Soon, he had graduated to making fish fry and chicken curry – and didn't he do it well ?

Even before Subramani had turned 18, he had become The Cook. It was a delight going to Subramani's mess. It used to be spotlessly clean. Each person was greeted with a warm smile and a naughty comment. "Check you waistline, *annai* (elder brother in Tamil)" ! he would shout out to Manoba and Philip, the two rotund brothers with an insatiable appetite, who worked in RTU and who always bullied Subramani, in a good-natured way, to let them taste his delightful food and that too, without paying for it ! Subramani would shoo them away and guard his 'mess' fiercely. Only those who paid and were eligible to eat in his mess as per RTU's criteria, would be served - and Manoba and Philip obviously did not qualify!

But he never forgot his own past. As and when new children, mostly orphans, were admitted to RTU's foster homes, Subramani would go and meet them, make friends with the new children and assure them that they would be happy in their new homes. He was extremely caring, going out to meet people who were unwell or in needed help. On days when visitors were expected, he felt doubly responsible to maintain high degree of hospitality. The food that day would be doubly delicious !

One of his fond recollections was about the time when a BBC team came visiting from London in 1990. The team of about 6 journalists and technicians who had come down to make a film on Bro. Kimpton's work were so touched by Subramani's hospitality that each day after their shoot, they would come and spend a few minutes with him, asking him questions which of course, he could not understand well. All that he understood was that they had named him 'Superman', partly because he worked so hard and partly because it was difficult for them to pronounce his name ! And that name came to stay for a long time. He was 'Superman' to many of his friends on the campus from then on.

But life moved on. Subramani, as was his nature, wanted to learn yet another skill. Three years in the mess and he was moved to the batik section where he learnt how to make lovely batik printed wall hangings and bed linen. He was even more delighted, for now, he had a provident fund account, was eligible to staff loan and was a member of the workers' association.

But all these days, in spite of his heavy work load, he had taken time out in the evenings to go to Raghavan, a school teacher, who had agreed to make him functionally literate. By the time Subramani moved to the batik unit, he had learnt basic reading and writing. He would try to read the newspaper headlines and even some simple story books and magazines. He had opened a bank account and was keen on savings. When he had saved enough, he bought 3 cents (100 cents make an acre) of land and with RTU's support, he built a small, one-bedroom house. The little Subramani, just in his early twenties now, was a proud home-owner and had taken his first step onto the property ladder ! It was indeed a proud day for him when most of his friends, staff of RTU, came for his housewarming.

A couple of months later, he was married to Mallika, one of the children from the foster homes (her mother was a foster mother). Subramani had come up in life with his hard work and was often quoted as an example, especially to the boys in the boys' hostel, on how one needed to learn to face up to life's challenges.

Subramani and Mallika now have a son, Mohan. And after all that Subramani has been through, one can be rest assured that life for Mohan will be very very different - and compared to that of his father, he will have a very privileged life, full of love, care and support !

18. Why children's participation ?

I remember the first time I was part of a discussion on "children's participation". This was when I had joined Plan International in 1998. Participation? For what? How? Children are children and hence they should be spending time in studying and playing, most people would think. This was a session where we were being persuaded to integrate children's perspectives in everything we did to enhance the quality of our programmes.

It was then that a series of trainings were planned to help us understand the concept better. We went to Kundapur in southern Karnataka, where The Concerned for Working Children (CWC), an organisation working on children's issues and their rights, was based. They had several years of experience of organising children and had been successful in getting adults around to accepting children as 'stakeholders'.

It was indeed amazing. Over a period of one week, we interacted with a group of children, all of whom were working children and hence had missed out largely on formal education opportunities. They were obviously from poor families. But one thing that was common among them was the courage and confidence with which they had organised themselves, articulating their views and concerns and more importantly, determined to identify more and more such children and form them into groups. These children would then regularly interact with adults in *panchayats* (local government), schools, at places of work, with parents – to ensure that children were heard. Some of them had even shared the dais with ministers, bureaucrats, film stars and other influential people to voice their concerns. Some of them were members of task forces and working groups at various levels to provide their inputs on major policy documents that would influence the lives of children. And some even had the opportunity to travel abroad and represent the concerns of working children in India. One of the important areas of their role was to work closely with the *panchayats* to ensure that these *panchayats* are child labour free - no mean achievement in a country where there are reportedly 100 million working children, according to some estimates !

It was the same enthusiasm that I saw among the children of Sangam Vihar, a slum settlement in New Delhi, where CASP, an NGO had been working for years. Over a period of time, they had decided to be more proactive and not depend upon their parents and other adults alone to move ahead in life. They started managing community libraries, spread health awareness messages, ensured that children who had dropped out of school returned and even raised sensitive issues such as drug abuse, discrimination against girl children and HIV/AIDS. They had organised themselves into *bal panchayats* (an informal forum for children, modelled on local government). They took pride in organising their annual child rights workshops where their counterparts from over 10 states would assemble in Delhi. They then had interactions with individuals from various walks of life who listened to their presentations and were asked to respond on specific issues.

I was once asked to be a respondent on one of the panels and let me assure you, it was quite an unnerving experience for me (I am sure the children noticed the discomfort and were pretty amused about it !). The issues they raised ranged from the reservation policy of the government (because of which quotas in educational institutions and jobs were created for people from certain communities that were considered to be socio-economically marginalised) to the inadequacy of government resources in promoting elementary education! And these were children who lived in settlements that were deprived of even the most basic facilities and belonged to families with very insecure livelihoods. Many of them were not even sure if they would continue their education because of economic compulsions on them to go out and earn to complement their families' income. But they had certainly arrived as thinking citizens !

I remember the time we asked the Samuha (one of the NGOs that Plan International partnered with) staff team to hold a consultation with children when they were planning a watershed development programme(which involved water harvesting and soil conservation to improve agriculture productivity) in some villages of Raichur district in Karnataka. They were not convinced at all in the first place. Children? And watersheds? It was a 'technical' programme, some said. "We work closely with the local community in planning any such programme, so why do we need to consult separately with children"? some others queried. "After all, wouldn't the adults be able to easily represent the views of children"?

But on our continued persuasion, they yielded and decided to give it an honest try. They met with small groups of children, for which, they got help from teachers, village workers and just about anyone who could help with this process. This went on for a few weeks. It did take some time for the children to warm up. After all, who would ever ask them for their views ? They were only told what to do and how, and rarely explained why ! The Samuha team also took some time to lose their inhibitions and communicate with children at their level. Gradually, they began seeing the results. "The men in our village would ask for timber trees, so that they can sell the wood and make money. The women in our village will ask for fodder trees and trees that can yield fuel. But as children, we want fruit trees. We barely get to eat fruits and we know some fruits can grow very well in our soil", they asserted strongly. They even seemed willing to do the work of planting fruit trees and tending them.

This then became an integral part of the programme. The local government school headmaster also agreed to allow fruit trees to be planted on the school grounds, which was otherwise hardly put to any use. Moreover, it was part of the area that constituted a 'watershed' under the programme. It took only some time for the Samuha team to recognise and appreciate the children's enthusiasm for the programme. They then held regular meetings, assign responsibilities amongst themselves and monitor progress. This became such an enthusing example that '*bal aranyas*' or children's forests became a regular part of Samuha's watershed development programme.

19. Training – with a difference

In spite of our conviction about the need for children to be heard, we were not sure about Lalitha's idea of a capacity building programme for children. Lalitha Iyer, our colleague, was a keen champion of children's right to participate in decision making. She had developed a module that would enable children develop their confidence to understand local issues and present it articulately to the adults in their community. But she was so clear about her ideas that we eventually invited her to conduct this programme in Myrada's (a Bangalore based NGO) project area in Mysore that we partnered   with.

It was a 2-week schedule, sometime in mid-2000. I accompanied Lalitha to Mysore and was there on the first day. It was a day of familiarisation. The children were there, about 20 of them from different villages. They seemed excited about this programme when they heard what it was about.

I then met the same group on the last day of the programme. The group had been completely transformed. The very same children who had been so reluctant and diffident on the first day were now ready to make a presentation to a group of adults including their parents. They huddled into groups and busied themselves for a presentation. They were to present their visions for their village. There was also the usual song, dance and drama played out, as normally happens during such occasions, but it was with a difference. These were now around social issues that were of concern to them – discrimination against the girl child, lack of education opportunities, working children, drug abuse, alcoholism, poor sanitation conditions and even on the indifference of government officials to their problems, all of which had been conceived, scripted, directed and   presented   by   these   children!

The parents who had assembled there could not believe that it was their children who were articulating on issues that they themselves did not have the confidence to. They swelled with pride. It was evident on their faces, in their smiles. They knew their families and their communities would never be the same again. A slow but sure process of transformation had started.

Sure enough, in less than 6 months' time, some of the children who had participated in the programme successfully negotiated with a local landlord with whom three children of the village worked as bonded labour and got them released, a feat that the adults had never managed to achieve down the generations!

20.   The unintended outcomes !

I have had the opportunities of visiting several villages and meeting several people on my field visits. Meeting children was very special, though. It was always a great delight to meet with children and interact with them. Their enthusiasm was infectious, their views were forthright. Talking to them invariably provided deep insights on the lives of people in these villages and the difference that development projects were making. It was indeed very encouraging to hear from them how their lives had changed for the better because of these projects – better drinking water and sanitation facilities, better schooling, improved health, more sources of income, higher level of awareness etc. But it was from the children that we also heard of some of the unintended outcomes of our programmes.

We once visited a village in a district in south India, which received poor rainfall. The project there focussed on supporting agricultural developments. It meant improving farm lands, conserving water, providing credit for seeds and fertilisers and training on improved agricultural practices, all of which would mean more acres of productive land and higher incomes.

One of the children we met was Senthil. He was about 14 and was working on a piece of land owned by his family. He met us with a broad grin. He and his father had been toiling since morning. It was all worth it, he felt. The vegetable crop was good. They had also planted some coconut trees which were growing steadily. Things had certainly looked up over the past 2 years. For the first time ever since he could remember, they were cultivating the land all year round, thanks to an irrigation tank which conserved enough water to meet the needs of the farmers whose farms were located in the vicinity.

"Do you go to school"? I asked Senthil. He looked up to his

father, as if seeking permission to reply. "How can he go?", his father, Murugappan asked. "There is now so much work on this farm, thanks to this project that has been implemented. Previously, a large portion of my land was fallow and no cultivation was possible, but things have improved and I want to make the most of this opportunity. If he goes to school, who will help me? I cannot afford to employ labour on my farm. His mother has to look after the home and attend to household chores. She also works in the local *anganwadi* (a government-run centre for pre-school age children) as a helper to make some extra income." We looked at Senthil. Probably sensing what our next question would be, he said, "I did go to school. I have completed standard 6 and I was reasonably good in studies. I was interested to continue. But then it is my duty to help my father and now there is so much work to do on the farm. So when he asked me to discontinue studying, I did. There was no option", he said nonchalantly. I could trace a tinge of bitterness, of regret, in his voice. Having gone to school and having been a good student, he was probably aware of the consequences of a choice he had to forego. Well, this is not what we hoped would happen with a project meant to raise incomes!

On another occasion, travelling through a drought prone region in south India, we met up with many people, trying to understand how the drought was affecting the local population. Most people had to depend on casual work as agricultural labourers to survive. Women and men worked side by side wherever they got an opportunity to work. A road construction, a pond renovation, a school building construction, well just about any work was welcome. Evenings were time to relax for the men. They would sit in the school veranda or under the banyan tree or in front of the temple, smoking *bidis*, exchanging notes for the day. Some extra bucks during the day also meant assembling at the local *arrack* shop to have a few intoxicating swigs.

For the women though, evenings meant phase two of their working day. Cooking their evening meal, collecting water, washing clothes, milking the cows and feeding them........their work never seemed to end. But then, they were also involved in something else. Every week, on a specific day, they would meet in groups of 10 or 15 or 20 at the most. They called themselves 'self-help groups'. Each group had a different name. Each meeting would last for about an hour. Money was collected towards their individual savings which was managed collectively, loans were disbursed and the weekly repayments were   transacted.

We attended one such meeting on a warm April evening. As usual, there was a group of curious children who had seated themselves a little away, watching intensely the activities of their mothers. Most of them were girls. The boys were busy playing at a distance. Most of the girls had a younger child on her hips or in her lap or clutching her hand. As the women dispersed and walked towards their homes, we went closer to the girls. On seeing us come towards them, they laughed nervously, moving closer to their mothers. Some of them even ran away. But with Anita (my colleague from Plan) beside us, we managed to hold back a smaller group of girls, most of whom   were   between   10-14   years   of   age.

"Do you know what your mothers were doing"? Anita asked. "Yes, they are collecting savings and giving loans". "Do you know why are doing so"? she asked. "Yes", one of them said. "So that we won't be dependent on the local moneylender for money and so that we can meet our needs better". Good, we thought. Here was the next generation of self-help group members.

We were just about to move on. "But I don't like what they are doing", one of girls said. We turned around in surprise. This 14-year old was Nirmala. She said, "It's all fine that we don't have to depend on a moneylender or even a bank for loans. But I don't like it". On being asked why she didn't like it, she said, "Our mothers have lot of work to do. They work in the fields or construction sites all day long. When they come home, they have lot of work. Our fathers don't help us. They while away their time talking or playing cards or drinking country liquor. So invariably, we end up doing a lot of work as our brothers too would not do household work. We need to fetch water, collect fuel wood, take care of our younger siblings, help in cooking......well, help in everything that our mothers do. Now they have even less time. They spend time in meetings, maintaining records, going to the bank, attending trainings or other meetings. This takes them to the block headquarters, 10 kilometres away. So while we think it is good for the family and the village, I think it is not good for the girls as they face additional burden - which means that some of us had also to drop out of school. I could not continue beyond standard 6. I know of other girls in the village too who have had similar problems. But girls normally don't speak out as it is anyway considered enough for girls to be educated till standard   5".

We listened to Nirmala in rapt attention. The other girls too listened carefully and seemed to agree with what she was saying. Nirmala had just explained to us the other side of a micro-credit programme that till then, we were unaware of. Probably their mothers (leave alone their fathers) too were unaware of this. Or even if they were aware, the benefits that this programme brought in as perceived by them probably was more substantial that what they perceived girls' education could do. Senthil and Nirmala had just made us aware of what we normally tend to overlook beyond the normal 'project outputs'.

21. Fostering – with love and care

From time immemorial, mothers have been epitomes of love and sacrifice. Ancient mythology and modern literature alike are full of stories of mothers whose boundless love for their children instilled humane values in them. While we do see mothers in our daily lives, in the family, among friends, neighbours, I have also met several women whose lives were full of challenges that would seem insurmountable – women with difficult husbands who are alcoholic, drug pushers, petty criminals, women who were widowed or deserted or abused, women who were engaged in backbreaking jobs on roads and buildings. But wherever they were, their primary concern was their children, most of whom would accompany them to places of their work. The challenges were multiplied if they had children who needed special attention – children with disabilities, children who were abused, children who were ill and malnourished.

It was this ability of women to love and care for children that Bro. Kimpton had faith in. He used to come in regular contact with children who were orphaned and abandoned, children in dire need, with nowhere to go. There was no way, in many cases, to trace their antecedents. He had just met one such woman. Rajammal, and he didn't know what he could do to support her.

It must have been in the late-sixties. One day, someone approached him with five children, siblings, who had lost their parents. They hailed from Kodaikanal, a beautiful town nestling in the Kodai hills of Tamil Nadu in south India, 60 kilometres from where Bro. Kimpton lived. He met them at the church, about 10 kilometers from where he stayed, where he used to go for his morning and evening prayers. When asked by the parish priest if he could take care of the children, he had no hesitation in refusing. He had a home for poor boys who lived in small cottages. All of them were poor, many of them were either orphans or had only one parent. They were aged 6-14. He had made arrangements for their stay and for them to go to the nearby government school. But here were five children, 2 of them girls, both of whom and a boy were below 6. They all looked very under nourished. They apparently had not been going to school. There was no way in which he could take care of them. But he prayed for them in the hope that some kind soul would take care of them. Somewhere in his mind though, the thought of these children troubled him. They looked so sad and miserable. But then, there was only this much one could do, he comforted himself.

The same evening, a frail young lady, probably in her mid-twenties, came to meet him. She had a child with her. She had been deserted by her husband or was probably a widow. She had nowhere to stay. Could she be accommodated somewhere? Could Bro. Kimpton take care of her? Well, the answer was simple. He couldn't. He just couldn't! He did not have a programme for destitute women. There was also the question of money. These were early days when he had not yet been able to identify enough sources of funds to support his activities on a regular basis.

Yet, he was perturbed. Something told him that he had not taken the right decision. He got on to his motorcycle and went to the top of a hillock nearby. He sat, lost in his own thoughts. An inner voice seemed to tell him, "Go, bring the children back with you. Keep them with you". His restlessness grew. He stayed on, trying to concentrate, to meditate and overcome his restlessness. A little later, he came down, got on to his motorcycle and went back to the church to meet the parish priest and tell him that he would take care of the children.

The priest was delighted. He accompanied the children to Bro. Kimpton's place in his jeep and saw off the children, content in the knowledge that they would be well taken care of. Bro. Kimpton was still unsure of what exactly he could do. He was certainly not in a position to take care of these children himself. That is when he remembered Rajammal, the woman who had come to him just a few days ago. She had been abandoned by her husband and she had come to Bro. Kimpton, seeking refuge as she has nowhere else to go. He found her easily. She was still around the place where Bro. Kimpton lived. He asked Rajammal, who was still waiting in the hope of getting some help from him. "Can you take care of these children if I give you a place to stay here", he asked. "Oh yes, readily", she replied, her eyes lighting up with joy and expectation. She saw a ray of hope in this unexpected question. If she had a place to stay, she could also see to it that her own child was secure! "But", Bro. Kimpton said, "I want you to be a mother to them. It's not just taking care of them, feeding them and attending to their needs. It is about giving them love. It is about caring for them as your own children", he said. She agreed readily, once again.

And that was the modest beginning of the foster family programme. As he got more support for the programme, he built small little houses as a dwelling unit for a woman who was called a 'foster mother'. These women came from poor backgrounds and were invariably single – widowed or destitute. Some of them also had their own children with them, and in addition, they cared for children who found their way to RTU – abandoned, orphaned, sick, disabled. Most children came at a very young age. In the area which was notorious for female infanticide, it was no surprise that most of the children were girls. Some of them were just a day old.

But however weak or disabled or difficult a child was, the foster mothers welcomed them happily and soon got down to the task of settling the children in their new homes. They would go about the usual ceremonies with great joy – naming ceremony, feeding ceremony, ear piercing, tonsuring....well, just about anything. And more importantly, they gave them love. They would often reflect on their past, about the difficult circumstances that brought them to RTU and feel content about the security of their new abode. When the children went to school, they would spend time in learning a new skill. They also got counselling support on parenting, as some children were indeed very difficult because of the traumas or shocks they had faced in their lives. And as the children grew into adolescence, there were new challenges to be faced. They also were conscious of the high degree of accountability expected of them, for they were dealing with the lives of these children. The way they brought them up and instilled values in them would ultimately determine the type of human beings they would grow up to in life.

Many children 'graduated' from the programme. Most of the teenagers, and especially the boys, moved out to a hostel as they were now old enough to take care of themselves. Eventually, the children who moved out of the programme got married, had children. But they could never actually sever the bond that existed between them and their foster mothers. Each vacation, they came home, to spend time with their mothers. Each time they came, they brought with them nice little gifts that their pocket money could afford. Each time their mothers fell ill, they would come to visit them. Marriages were of course only with the blessings of these foster mothers, who often then took leave to oversee the delivery of their daughters or daughters-in-law.

It may sound like romanticizing. It may also seem like 'gender stereotyping', of women being seen prominently as 'care givers'. But then, this was different. These were women who were not just doing a 'job', which they could well get away with. Most of them had invested much more into this 'job'. They had invested tons of love and care, a true tribute to humanity !

22. Kesarbai, the pioneer, leads the way

It was not easy getting to the villages of Chindwada district (in central Madhya Pradesh, India), famously known as 'Kamalnath's constituency'. (Kamalnath is a senior and an influential leader of the Congress Party). As we wound our way through the rough tracks, we rocked in the jeep. But Yaseen's expert driving assured us a safe passage. The landscape was dotted with teak trees growing on forest lands. The streams were running, thanks to the good rains. The fields seemed to be buzzing with activity. The seeds had already germinated and the fresh growth provided these fields with a velvety green cover. A variety of crops were being grown – maize, sorghum, pearl millets, paddy, groundnut and even cotton and sugarcane. There were small beds of vegetable crops too. There was an upbeat mood all around and why not? The rain gods had been generous, ponds and small dams were full of water, people had enough work on their farms and were looking   forward   to   a   good   harvest.

I was traveling to Chindwada in 1995. One of ActionAid's partner NGOs, Prayas, worked in a few villages of this district, in the Amarwara and Harrai blocks. As we passed through the villages, girls and boys, women and men waved and shouted out aloud to Sadiq and Seema, who waved back cheerily. "Aren't you going to stop here"? they asked as the jeep slowed down to acknowledge their greetings. "Why aren't you coming to our village"? they queried. Sadiq and Seema were a familiar sight in these villages. Both were post graduates in social work and had been working with the local community, predominantly *adivasis* (tribals), since the late eighties. "No", they replied. "This time, we are going to Jhirna. It's a long time since we went there, and, as you know, Kesarbai will be very upset if we put off our visit to her village once again". "Yes of course", they nodded knowingly. They knew Kesarbai too, very well indeed. After all, she was one of them.

The people of Jhirna saw the familiar sight of the Mahindra Commander jeep from a distance and as we approached the village, we were surrounded in no time. "*Namaste*", they shouted aloud, "Welcome, welcome, we were wondering what took you so long to come", they chorused. As we unwound and tumbled out of the jeep wondering if our backs were alright after the rough drive, we saw a frail looking lady in a bright orange coloured saree with colourful flowers printed all over, coming towards us making her way through the crowd. She had a neat line of vermillion in the parting of her hair which was tied neatly in a tight knot. In spite of her frame, she seemed to exercise some authority as she surged ahead of the crowd. "This is Kesarbai", Seema introduced proudly. Seema had been instrumental in working with the women, organising them into groups and guiding them in managing village level initiatives such as forming grain banks, seed banks and cash savings so that they were not dependent on the local moneylenders who were highly exploitative. She had also trained them in legal awareness and with the help of her lawyer sister Sunita and husband Sadiq, had represented

91

many a case of harassment of the local people by the local authorities.

Kesarbai grinned. She was quite happy to see us. Each time Seema and Sadiq came to her village, there was something to discuss, there was some new information to be gained, there was some more impetus to the village works. This time too, she had something important to discuss, and something else to share.

As Kesarbai called out to the people around her, they started assembling in the courtyard of one of the houses nearby. The women huddled together in one corner of the open space, while the men seated themselves at the other end. *Bidis* (tobacco rolled in the locally available *tendu* leaves, for smoking) came out and the air was thick with its smell. There was an excited chatter. It was about 7 in the evening then and the women had ensured that they had cooked their evening meal before coming for this meeting. They wanted to discuss the plans for a new programme in the village that would improve their lands and help them conserve water. The men had some good ideas, but they wanted the women to put these forth, as the women apparently enjoyed better 'credibility', largely because of the way their '*sangathan*' (association) had been functioning ! Also, they had such an impressive record of managing the grain bank, the seed bank and their savings, which the men just could not match up to.

There was nothing special about Kesarbai, in a sense. Like the other 40 odd families living in the village, hers was also a simple *adivasi* family. She had been married for about 30 years now. Life had been full of struggles. She used to spend long hours in the farm, alongside her husband. She would tend the cows, in addition to attending all the domestic chores. Like the other women in her village, she took pride in keeping her house clean, applying fresh coats of cow dung in the '*angan*', (courtyard) making small paintings in bright colours on the walls of the veranda. Her kitchen was bare and simple, but spotlessly clean. Her grains had been stored away with great care   to   last   the   whole   year.

The monsoon months were very busy with work on the farm. Her husband would often sleep in the farm during the nights when the crop was ready, like the other men in the village. Kesarbai grew vegetables in a small plot of land just behind her house. But once the crops were harvested and stored, there was not much to do. Well, she could still grow some vegetables in her '*baadi*' (kitchen garden), but that did not need much time. And like other women and men, she too would look for opportunities for employment – on road sites, dam sites, making small bridges and causeways, well, just about any public work that came her way. After all, it meant an additional Rs. 20 per day for each day of work. Even if it was backbreaking, and even if it meant so much of additional work, it was important to keep the family together, ensuring that there was enough for the whole family to eat and making ends meet. She could also not rely entirely on her husband. Lazy as he was, he was not keen to find work for himself. He often found it too much to do. Moreover, even if he did manage to find work and earn something, most of it was spent on buying the local country liquor, like most other men. Most of them would then create a scene in the village, by picking up fights with their neighbours, beating their wives, shouting at their children, cursing the landlord, well, just about anything that they felt like doing that day, promptly to be forgotten at the   break   of   dawn   the   next   day   !

In March, Kesarbai, like the other women, would wake up early in the morning, before daybreak, to join a group of women who would go to the forests nearby to collect '*mahua*' (found in the spring season) flowers. This would then be bought   by   local   traders   and   among   other things, *mahua* flowers would be used for making the local brew. There was a good demand for this. They would collect the flowers that were shed, from the ground under the trees. The more enterprising ones would even climb the trees to pluck the flowers. Kesarbai could do that, and she quite enjoyed it also. But it had its own hazards. Many a time, women had fallen from these trees, causing bruises and injuries. The fact that they were climbing the trees wearing *sarees* did not really help. But then, in the company of the women at dawn, partially assisted by the dark and with no one else watching, they would lift their *sarees* knee length, take one end of it between their legs and tuck it at the waist behind, to make it look almost like a *dhoti* that the men wore, which was more comfortable for climbing. But what they feared was the leopards (*tendua*, as they called them) and the occasional bears that they would encounter. Which is why, they would always go in a group.

The *mahua* season would last for about 2 weeks. They wished they could store the *mahua* flowers so that it could fetch up to Rs. 15 per kilo. But then, the need for hard cash during a season when work on the agricultural fields was low, meant that they would sell it to the local traders, who would anyway have done their rounds well before the *mahua* season had set in and pay them an advance to ensure that the women sell all the *mahua* to them. It was in a way, trying to capture the source. Well, why then would they accept this advance and be bound to sell to the trader, one could ask. The answer was simple – the need for liquid cash ! Most of the families grew crops during the monsoon season and harvest it at the onset of winter. Most of it was kept for their home consumption though. Anyway, it wouldn't last the whole year. Most would have to buy grains and other food items on credit, paying huge interest, though. There was hardly any marketable surplus. Thus, to them, the local traders came across as being benevolent, for they were advancing money against the crop (*mahua* flowers) which had not yet been collected. But what they did not realize was that their collection was bought at rock bottom rates, sometimes as low as Rs. 2, which could then be sold for prices that would be 7-10 times more. !

Kesarbai had often wondered if there was a way out. Somehow, it was to do with non-availability of liquid cash, she knew. But she was not clear how this could be tackled. And it was also to do with poor yields from their farms. But then, what could be done about that? The *mahua* season was a given too.   No   one   could   extend   that!

That was when she came to Amarwara to meet Seema at her office. Seema and Sadiq had, in the mid-eighties, set up an organisation, Prayas, to work with the tribal communities in Chindwada district, setting up a small office in Amarwara, about 40 kilometres from Chindwada. Kesarbai was accompanied by three other women from her village.

"We heard that you are working with women like us and forming '*sangathans*' (associations) in the village. We want to do something similar so that we can tide over our problems", she said, very simply. She had certainly come with lot of expectations, but with little hope. Hadn't she done the rounds at the various government offices – the Block Development Office, the Education office, the Health centre, the Water department's office, for various purposes? And what the response? Almost always, it was of no use! Which made even the men of her village jeer at her. "We told you nothing will happen in this village. You are being unrealistic by visiting these *babus* (officials). You need to pay them money, you foolish woman", they would mock her. "Only then will they respond to our problems". "But at least, I try", she would retort back, "unlike you who are content at accepting things lying down, blowing away our earnings with your *bidis* and drinking away your earnings with the country liquor" ! While it was all very frustrating, deep inside, she knew that somewhere, sometime,   her   perseverance   would   pay.

But Seema's response took her by complete surprise – a very pleasant surprise. "We are willing to help those who help themselves", Seema told her, which was something that rather baffled Kesarbai. Seema continued, "We don't want people to depend on us. We believe that you all have the power within to change your lives. Why don't you organise the women in your village and start a group activity, like initiating savings. You could save in whatever form and in whichever way you want. You can save through cash, food grains, seeds, and even *mahua* flowers. One of you should take the responsibility to keep track of who has saved and how much has been saved. We will help you with that", she said. Kesarbai shook her head vigourously in agreement. This was certainly making a lot of sense to her. But she looked at her friends who had accompanied her, seeking their endorsement. "If you have understood what madam said and if it is ok with you, it is ok with us too", they had said. They had faith and confidence in Kesarbai. Many a time, Kesarbai had come up with simple solutions to complex problems. They were sure that this time too, Kesarbai would come up with something useful.

Kesarbai did not lose much time in organising a women's meeting. Not that it was easy. She still staved off delirious comments from the men, including her husband. Some of the other women were admonished by their husbands when they said they were going for a meeting. Some were horrified that their women also seemed to go the Kesarbai way ! But then, the women were undaunted. The first meeting had over 20 women, just a little over half the number of women. But it was a good start, they thought.

"If we consume all that we have, all that we produce, we won't have anything when there is a crisis. So let us kept aside a little of what we have, each day, day after day. One of us will take the responsibility of calling meetings of our group, someone will take the responsibility of maintaining accounts", Kesarbai explained. There was quite a bit of animated discussion around the group. "Kesarbai, what are you talking about? Don't you know about us already? We barely have enough to eat and feed the family. How do you expect us to save from this"?

It was indeed a sobering thought. "We have to save", Kesarbai said slowly, with determination. "Sisters, there is no way out. We need to sacrifice. I know it's difficult. But we won't die if we eat a little less, each day. After all, it is for a better future. Each day, when you sit down to cook your meal, keep a '*muthi*' (fistful) of grain aside in a '*kothi*' (an earthen storage bin). Let me tell you, it won't hurt...at all ! Slowly, start talking to your husbands. They also need to know, to understand, and to co-operate. And every week, let us deposit the grain thus saved into a common *kothi*. I will ask one of the men to spare their *kothi*. Ramlal has some spare *kothis*. I will talk to him", she said. "What will we do with the stored grain?", one of the women asked. "When our own *kothis* are empty, we will take some grain from the *kothi* and put it back with some extra quantity when we can repay. If we borrow 1 kilo, we will repay a kilo and 200 grams. That way, our stock will increase. And then, no one will go hungry in our village, and equally, we will not fall prey to the moneylenders or local traders who charge high   interest   rates".

The women brightened up. It certainly sounded very interesting. "Why don't we also save some cash"? one of the women suggested. There were soft giggles of disbelief around. "Hey you, do you have that much of extra cash for you to save" ? The women laughed ! But not Kesarbai. She said, "Jamna is not wrong. Can we not think of saving a couple of rupees a week ? If 20 of us save Rs. 2 per week, we will have Rs. 40 each week in a common fund. And that will become Rs. 160 per month. Now, isn't that a decent amount? If someone falls ill and wants some money urgently, or wants to buy food urgently, can we not lend at an interest rate which is lower that the local *sahukars*'(traders) "? she asked. The women were quiet. This too made sense. "Okay sisters, it is getting quite late and before our husbands start shouting and abusing us for what they would call gossiping, let us get back to our homes. I am sure we all have work to do. But think about what we have discussed carefully and let us meet again next week, may be the day after the weekly *haat* (market)", she said.

The women dispersed. But there was a strange sense of excitement. As they wound through the dark lanes in twos and threes, they could not conceal the excitement. They felt that they were embarking upon something that would change their lives. Even the thought of an angry husband or hungry, squealing children waiting to be attended to did not seem to dampen   their   enthusiasm!

This meeting had indeed changed the perspective of these women, most of whom had always believed that nothing much could change in their lives. Slowly, but with determination and amidst a great deal of cynicism especially from their men folk, the women started meeting regularly, saving fistfuls of grain and a little amount of cash. Seema and Sadiq were impressed.

In a short span of 6 months, the women had not just shown their desire to take control of their lives, but had been very systematic about it. They would travel to Tinsai, a village a little away from theirs, where the women had initiated something similar a couple of years earlier. They wanted to learn. They wanted to know more. Keeping accounts was their biggest problem. They got the primary school teacher to help them and hoped that over a period of time, one of their school going girls will be capable enough to take on this task. They had also managed to impress upon their men to think of other ways   to   develop   themselves.

The men, not to be left behind, started discussing about the prospects of improving their lands and constructing small earthen structures to conserve rainwater, which could be used when their wells had gone dry or the monsoon had receded. Seema and Sadiq had agreed to send their engineer over to their   village   to   firm   up   their   plans.

As the *mahua* season approached, Kesarbai and the rest of the members asked Seema if her organisation could lend them money equal to what they would otherwise have earned if they had sold the *mahua* produce to the local traders. It did not amount to much, but it was a critical need. Seema agreed. The women got some liquid cash, which enabled them to store the *mahua* flowers. They could now wait for another 3-4 months for the prices to rise and then sell it at a profit. Which they did, and in style! Each time one of them went to the market, they would   check   out   the *mahua* prices.   As   the *mahua* season receded, the price started going up. Then, in the month of

June, they decided to sell the *mahua* flowers. The prices had gone up considerably by then. Moreover, they had the additional problem of storing the flowers through the monsoon, which was difficult. On one of the market days, the women took their produce to the market in bullock carts and weren't they proud to be a seller in the off-season rather than a buyer, something which they had never dreamt of? And they had reasons to be happy, because their men folk had also been equally enthusiastic and supportive, casting away their earliler scepticism as they had now begun to see a reason behind what they   were   doing   !

They came back from the market, with Kesarbai securely tying up the cash with a knot at the edge of her *saree* which she then tucked it safely round her waist. It was not just her money – it belonged to many of them and she had to be doubly careful! Before doing so, she had made sure that the women who accompanied her had counted the money and knew how much they had made. Next day, in the afternoon, they sat with the school teacher to work out the economics of this 'enterprise'. They calculated the costs of the gunny bags which were bought to take the flowers, the amount they paid for the bullock cart, and even the couple of teas and snacks they had while trying to sell their produce. The result – a net profit of a little over 100%, something that the best businesses would envy them for! It was time for celebration. That evening, they had a feast. It was a community event. Some made maize *rotis*, some cooked the rice. There were aubergines, potatoes, onions and green chillis for the vegetables and the curries. And there was chicken ... hot, spicy chicken! The local brew made from *mahua* was quite prominent too! Men and women alike indulged in celebrating this important event. For once, no one was complaining about drinking!

23. The tale of three brothers

This should have been the tale of five brothers, much like the mythological Pandavas (except that they had two sisters too). They even had a step-brother (like Karna, the half-brother of the Pandavas). But here, I will restrict it to three of them. The trio had a lot in common – all the three are very outgoing, extremely warm and helpful, caring, love children and music. Each one of them have very special skills. The eldest, Arumugam (all names have been changed), could write plays, choreograph and compose folk songs. The next in line, Suresh, was quite an all-rounder, adept at electric repairing, carpentry, plumbing, driving and many other skills, very deft and quick with his hands and very agile. Vijay, the youngest, was more similar to Suresh, though less focussed, and was probably as good as Suresh in most of the skills, except that he could also handle computers quite well. All the three barely had a proper formal education beyond their 10th class. Arumugam, being more academically inclined, pursued his studies intermittently through evening classes and distance education, to eventually obtain a Masters degree. I first met them in 1989. Arumugam is now in his early sixties, Suresh in his mid-fifties and Vijay a few years younger. All the three are married and have children. Arumugam is now a grandfather. So, what's the story of their lives ?

Arumugam, being the oldest, still has vivid memories of their childhood. Theirs was a riches-to-rags story. Arumugam's father was a widower who married his mother a few years after the death of his first wife, from whom he had a son. His sister preceded him in coming to this world. He was followed by four brothers and a sister. Vijay was the youngest of the lot. Their father was quite a well known person in Madurai. He was very active in the then flourishing Tamil theatre, before Tamil cinema snuffed out competition from the theatre. His father wrote plays and directed them, many of which ran to packed houses. His father, a strong Congress supporter, was also known as a speech writer for prominent Tamil Congressmen in the 1940's and 1950's. Arumugam remembers that his huge house, symbolic of their prosperity, was always filled with people from the fields of theatre and politics. His mother had a tough time in extending hospitality to all those who came to meet his father. As his father's popularity increased, he was also asked to be the scriptwriter for a Tamil film. They led quite a comfortable and occasionally luxurious lifestyle. Food and clothing was aplenty and never a cause for concern. Though from a family who were traditional goldsmiths, many of whom had thriving businesses, Arumugam's father did not consider taking up his traditional occupation, for what he did in the art and creative world gave him a lot of satisfaction, fame and popularity.

Things changed all of a sudden with the demise of Arumugam's father. Life came to standstill for this family. His mother, who had spent most of her time within the four walls of the house, looking after a large family and the numerous guests, was at crossroads. Bringing up seven of her own children and a stepson for someone who had no formal education and who had no experience of managing money was a huge uphill task. Soon on hearing about his father's demise, Arumugam remembers people queuing up asking for the repayment of loans they claimed they had extended to his father. It was impossible for a widow to stave them off. With the help of some family friends, she sold the house and most of their material possessions to pay off the family debts, while trying to reconstruct life for the family. Vijay and Suresh barely remember those days. Arumugam himself had just then stepped into his adolescence.

The following years were marked with struggle for survival. Even with plenty of family friends and relatives around, the going was not easy, for when it came to money, there was not much help that was forthcoming. Their mother did a variety of odd jobs and errands to keep the family from starvation. She also tried her hand at petty businesses. Arumugam started working as a helper in some shops that one of his father's friends was familiar with. Between him and his mother, they ensured that the younger siblings went to school while Arumugam dropped out of education.

But the struggle for survival was taking its toll on Arumugam's mother's health. She became increasingly weak with constant attacks of fever and cough. She started losing weight. Eventually, she was diagnosed as suffering from the dreaded tuberculosis. With hardly any money for good medical treatment, she was admitted to the district government hospital in Madurai. She could not hold on for long. Arumugam was eighteen when his mother died and Vijay, the youngest was only six. Arranging a decent cremation was itself a huge task. The owner of the rented house they lived in refused to let them bring his mother's dead body inside the house for the last rites. They finally had to take her body to a family friend's house with great difficulty. The years of struggle and his mother's illness meant that they were left with hardly any material possession, having had to sell most of their meagre possessions to survive. A little bit of cash and tiny pieces of gold ornaments that their mother had carefully kept aside had come in handy for their elder sister's marriage. The burden of taking care of his four younger brothers and a sister was now squarely on Arumugam's frail shoulders. Determined though he was to ensure that his siblings could continue their education, he was quite overwhelmed by the challenge.

As he looked around for opportunities, he came across Boys' Village, a home for orphaned and destitute children in Madurai district. Arumugam got his younger brothers admitted as boarders in the village. That was a great relief. All children from the boys' village went to the local government school, which meant that his brothers could continue with their education. When they grew older, they would graduate to Boys' Town, where, in addition to their formal education, they could also get a formal training in various vocational skills that would ensure that they could identify appropriate livelihood options. Arumugam himself managed to find himself the job of a typist in the Boys' Town and with that earning, he could take care of his sister (who would eventually qualify as a teacher). Suresh and Vijay learnt various skills – carpentry, electric wiring, lathe machinery etc., adept as they were with their hands. Arumugam, in addition to his typing, got involved with the programmes. His love for children meant that he would often spend time teaching the children, playing with them and engaging them with various hobbies, music and singing being his favourite.

Arumugam continued to develop himself. He got seriously involved with education programmes. He read voraciously to develop insights into child psychology and other dimensions of education. He enrolled himself for various training opportunities that came his way, which Boys' Town was willing to sponsor. When Bro. Kimpton set up Reaching the Unreached (RTU) as an independent organisation, moving away from his base in Boys' Village in the early eighties, Arumugam joined him and helped him with various administrative functions. He moved on to initiate RTU's education programmes and eventually headed the department, which, in a decade's time, provided quality education to over 2,000 children, in addition to imparting vocational skills to adolescent girls and boys. Some of the vocations included the more modern ones such as screen printing and computers. All this time, Arumugam continued to enrich his academic base, enrolled himself for various distance education courses and obtained a Masters in Sociology.

Arumugam's brothers charted their own course. Suresh joined one of the local contractors and worked as an electrician, plumber, motor mechanic and carpenter, all rolled in one. His cheerful disposition, his deft skills and his athleticism made him a very popular person. He was especially popular with the children in the foster homes which he would often visit to check on maintenance works. Like Arumugam, he too was very fond of children and had a very special way of getting along with them. Moreover, he was a good singer and could play percussion instruments quite well and that ensured that he was always there to participate in various entertainment programmes (which invariably would be co-ordinated or conceived by Arumugam, who would anyway be at the forefront). His dedication and commitment, and his sense of discipline were noticed. He was soon heading RTU's maintenance department, supervising the work of several technicians to ensure that the sprawling RTU campus, the staff houses, the foster homes, the many schools, the work sheds and other parts of the campus were fully functional.

Vijay was the proverbial black sheep of the family. As the youngest, he also probably took liberty. Having been orphaned at the age of six and with not much of disciplining early in his life, he tended to be wayward. He always had a tendency of not taking life seriously in general – which meant that he did not concentrate on his studies, nor did he pay much attention to relationships. He was, like Suresh, very adept at picking up skills though. And like Arumugam and Suresh, he was intrinsically a warm, loving and caring person. However, his waywardness put him in the wrong company. His late teens and his early twenties saw him leading a risky life, engaging in street fights, drinking at will and blowing away his earnings on movies, food and other forms of indulgence. He had a small job working in a unit that made steel cupboards. But the work was irregular. I believe there were times when he was out of work and went without proper food for several days. Though he worked in Madurai, I used to meet him often when he would come to visit Arumugam and Suresh in RTU. He soon became very attached to us.

In mid-1993, my wife and I moved to Delhi. The same year, in winter, he came to visit us in Delhi. It was meant to be a fortnight's stay. He apparently missed us and wanted to spend some time with us. While he was with us, I learnt that he had been out of work for quite some time. Frustrated in his attempt to find some work, he had decided to take a break. He came to Delhi with some cash that he borrowed from a friend, in the hope that on returning to Madurai, he would find a job and pay him back. Hearing that, I asked him to stay back in Delhi, assuring him that we would find a way to pay his friend back. Instead, I asked him to learn driving and learn Hindi. In three months' time, I was supposed to set up ActionAid's regional office for Madhya Pradesh in Bhopal. I was hopeful that I could find something useful for him to do there.

Vijay was a quick learner. He learnt Hindi. Moving around Delhi on his own boosted his confidence (he had never been beyond any south Indian state earlier). And he learnt driving too. When we moved to Bhopal in April 1994, he came with us. He was, in many ways, my Man Friday. There was a lot of work involved in setting up a new office. He did an excellent job of supporting Prahlad, our Administrative Assistant. In no time, he had explored Bhopal's roads and could take us anywhere, largely due to Prahlad's constant guidance. But more importantly, he started taking interest in ActionAid's work and development work in general. Often, he would sit in various meetings and workshops, trying to understand what development work meant. Often, he asked many pertinent questions. And when he got time, he would also try his hand at the computer (something that I didn't encourage him at that stage, honestly, fearing that our only PC could break down if not handled well).

A year later, I thought it was time for him to move. He was becoming too dependent on us, which was not healthy for him. That was the time a friend of mine was looking for someone like Vijay, which incidentally came up in one of our casual conversations. We discussed and agreed that Vijay could move to Chennai. In addition to his being trained for the job, it could, in the long run, be beneficial to Vijay too, considering that he hailed from Tamil Nadu. And it would also mean that he could start living independently.

Vijay made his mark in Chennai. He was quite popular with the team. He gradually began engaging himself with mainstream development work. That was the time when the organisation in Chennai had manage to rope in prominent Tamil filmstars (Suhasini, Revathy, Manorama) to do a film on *panchayati raj* (political decentralisation) that required lot of outdoor shooting. A film buff to the core, Vijay enjoyed this phase and very enthusiastically worked with the film technicians. All the time, he continued to explore ways to improve himself. He had mastered basic computer operations and became quite adept at surfing the net. He enrolled for a course and learnt the basics of computer hardware, enough for him to start assembling PCs on his own and selling it !

But the highpoint of his career, I think, came when he was asked to get involved in a programme for the homeless in Chennai and working with commercial sex workers' of Chennai to enable them explore other livelihood options. It meant late nights and lot of additional work. It meant lot of local travel. It meant rushing people to hospitals or negotiating with the local police. That's where probably the challenges he faced earlier on in life, came in handy. These were not situations that deterred him. In fact, he relished these opportunities.

When I met him at the World Social Forum in Mumbai in January 2004, he was a proud man. He introduced me to a group of sex workers with whom he had been working. He proudly showed the bank pass books these women were maintaining and explained the various processes he was engaged in rehabilitating these sex workers. The women too were very happy about all that Vijay had done and there was a certain bonding. Vijay had arrived, truly arrived !

24. Rituals – inaugurations !

The housing programme of Reaching the Unreached (RTU - where I worked for 4 1/2 years in the Southern Indian state of Tamil Nadu) was very popular. A specialist team of masons and carpenters had, over a period of time, been trained from among the local population. Every year, about 300 houses were built for people from the economically weaker sections. There was an elaborate process of selection of families to ensure that the programme was well targeted. Women headed households (who were either widows or deserted women), old aged and those with disabilities got preference. Most of the houses were constructed on plots of land that had been allocated to the landless, while some were on lands that had been bought or previously owned by these families. A community meeting preceded the process of identifying individual families. Once this process was over, there was a meeting to plan the layout of the village so that the houses were constructed in neat rows, which meant of course that some families had to let go a portion of their land to make way for a small path in between rows of houses. Once the construction was over, it had almost become mandatory for them to plant a coconut tree. "A coconut tree is as dear to us as a son", some of them would say.

What marked any housing programme in a village was the inauguration of the construction work and then, the inauguration of the newly built settlement. These rituals could compete with any of the local festivities (there were numerous, anyway !) in terms of the enthusiasm of the people, the colour, the gaiety and fervour. Costs for hosting these functions was through community contribution. The inauguration of the construction work was a quieter occasion though. Calendars were pored through to identify the 'auspicious' time, which was critical for such occasions. *'Rahu kaalam'* (the inauspicious periods in a day as per the Hindu calendar) was consciously avoided. The village would have an air of expectation. Walking through haphazard rows of thatched hutments with '*kolam*' (floral patterns in white commonly laid in front of homes on the ground) decorations as signs of welcome all along, we would be escorted to one of the spots where, in a matter of four weeks, a brand new house would stand ! That place, the chosen place, would be cleaned up. All the required implements and materials would be there – a spade, a bucket of water, *kumkumam* (vermillion), *chandanam* (sandal), a traditional brass lamp, *agarbatti* (incense sticks), coconuts, lemon, camphor, matchbox, pretty much everything that was needed. No inauguration would be complete without Bro. Kimpton being there (who would then negotiate to ensure that there are not blaring loudspeakers, so common on such occasions, to which he was truly allergic).

The inauguration would start with the lighting of the lamp and the *agarbattis*, lighting the camphor on top of a coconut which then would be held by a senior member of the construction team (and someone who was comfortable with the sequence and performance of the ritual) and swayed in a clockwise direction, facing the east, as was appropriate. That done, it was time to break the coconut on the spade, sprinkle its water around, moisten the hard earth with some more sprinkling of water and then calling upon one of the senior members from the community (which normally would mean an able bodied elder or '*thalaivar*') to take the spade, invoke the blessings of the gods who may then confer upon this community peace and joy in the new settlement. There would normally be a spontaneous round of applause once the spade comes hitting the earth making a deep dent depending upon how softened the earth was and how hard the blow was, the applause mostly being sustained by a crowd of excited children, who would by then have realized that the time for them to attack the packs of boiled candies that Bro. Kimpton would religiously bring with him on such occasions, was drawing excitingly near ! The women meanwhile would simultaneously go into ululating. In some cases though, in case of those communities not used to applauding, it would require a clarion call by one of the elders (*Enna, kaiyye thattunguda* ....c'mon guys, applaud !) who would call out loudly and exhort his ilk to follow suit. Of course, it was entirely another matter that the applause would continue till such time the same elder called it to a halt ! By then, the kids would have got dangerously near to the tray in which lay the packets of colourful boiled candies, looking very inviting in the morning sun. Barely would the first candy have dropped out of the now torn packet, than the kids would pounce as if on cue to grab their share of the goodie. What then came were the tiny glasses of sugary tea or tender coconuts, depending upon what was available and the biscuits, which would most likely find its way back to the bunch of excited children !

The construction work for a village would take roughly four weeks. The programme was so well orchestrated through experience that the five teams of masons and five teams of carpenters moved around from house to house in a predetermined sequence, before which, the community would have sorted out tricky issues of alignment of houses, laying out the common path and digging the foundation. Bricks, tiles, cement, sand, wood, lime, nails and the rest all seem to come in right in time when they are required, which often made me wonder why such things don't happen in the big cities where these and many other resources can be accessed so much faster and better ! And that too without sophisticated management tools like PERT charts or GANNT charts !!! All the men and women at work were from the local villages. About 1,500 people benefited directly from these works every year (which also included those from the brick kilns, bullock cart owners, the whitewashers and painters etc).

One of the masonry contractor teams was headed by a woman, who got into the job when her husband who managed one such team died suddenly. She had, in a very short period, very skilfully slipped into her husband's role, establishing her command over the rough and tough bunch of masons and carpenters, all men and thus felling a male bastion. Rajamma was her name. Not once did the fact that she was a woman, came in the way of her effectiveness and her ability to deliver quality work on time ! That probably prompted some other women to come forth and be trained as masons, which was yet again, a male bastion !

Coming back to the work, the neat row of white houses measuring about 200 square feet each with the beautiful earth coloured Managalore tiles and blue doors and window seemed to spring up as if from nowhere and would become the envy of the passers by who would stop, turn around, to look at this beautiful settlement that came up to replace the barely liveable huts. And, there was also a community hall and a threshing floor. The community hall was normally open from all sides with neat little pillars holding up the Mangalore tiled roof. That would become the venue of several meetings, functions, marriages, games and bc the centre of the community's life. The threshing floor was basically a raised platform that would cater to the needs of the families to dry their paddy.

The inauguration of the housing settlement, that is, once the entire work was over, was a time of great rejoicing. It was popularly referred to as 'paal kaachal' (boiling the milk which is an integral part of a housewarming ceremony), a ritual considered auspicious and mandatory in many parts of south India before one moves into a new house. Communities would try to be as creative as possible in putting up a 'good show'. Invariably, the loudspeaker on this instance, could not be ignored. It was a very important part of the ceremonies to enable the 'VIPs' make their two-bit speeches (which Bro. Kimpton was averse to...I mean, even the speeches. Many a time, it used to be a straight and simple 'vanakkam' which meant 'greetings', the Tamil equivalent of 'namaskar', followed by a 'nandri' which meant 'thank you'). Almost all the houses would have the welcoming kolam in front of their houses, sometimes colourful, but mostly in intricate patterns of white. The lanes would be decorated with rows of leaves strung to strings or with banana leaves bunched together. Banana leaves were an important of the function. These too were considered as auspicious.

The communities took these functions, especially the one to mark the completion of the construction work, very seriously. Though nothing was specifically designated, there was a pattern in the way responsibilities were designated. The men did the collection of money, buying of gifts (yes, there would be small gifts too....more about it later), and generally deciding the sequence of events including the spot where the function would be held and in some cases, the house where a 'symbolic' *paal kaachal* would be held. (It was not because the women couldn't do it or were not interested in. It's just that they didn't have the time. The men had the time a little more liberally allotted to them for reasons that are well known !). The women would ensure that the 'content' part of the ritual was taken care of. *Kolams* had to be organized. A check had to be kept on all the *puja* materials – the *kumkumam, chandanam*, flowers, coconuts, bananas, coconut leaves, coconuts etc. And yes ! They had to ensure that their best saree was well in shape to be worn on that special occasion which would mark their entry into their new home !

The youth's activities were generally centred around logistics. The guy responsible for the public address system had to be co-ordinated. They had to ensure that this guy brings with him the cassettes of the latest film songs that were a rage at that point in time. They had to ensure that there were a few songs which were picturised on specific rituals in the Tamil films, to get in that very special flavour of the occasion. And then, when the guests had come and were seated, they had to break open the soda bottles by pushing the marble that was stuck to the neck of the soda bottle to keep the gas intact, resulting in a conspicuous '*whoooossh*' sound of the escaping gas. Or they had to ensure that there were enough bottles of 'colour' (the local term used for a range of spurious soft drinks available aplenty in the country side at extremely affordable rates, packaged to mimic popular but more expensive brands such as Mirinda and Pepsi, sometimes, in the same Mirinda and Pepsi bottles that were surreptitiously bought over by these mini bottling plants) were available. The popular choice among the 'guests' (which was more to politely avoid being treated to sodas and 'colours' of suspect quality) was tender coconuts – in which case those from the village, who loved these sodas and bottles of 'colours', would generously treat themselves to these fizzy drinks. There would be some snacks too. Glucose biscuits which could easily pass off as the very popular 'Parle Glucose Biscuits' but which, on closer scrutiny, would actually be something as close as 'Parel' biscuits or some such spurious name, were pretty common. Also in the mix of treats was some local 'mixture' (a spicy, savoury snack), which was usually very tasty.

Identification of the guests to be invited was also an elaborate process that required a series of community level discussions. There would be usual suspects from RTU. Bro. Kimpton was a must. Many inaugurations were put off by a few days, or even a few weeks, to ensure that he was around (which he normally was, except in May when he would spend a couple of weeks in Kodaikanal on his retreat). Bro. Kimpton, the '*Berther*' or the '*ayya*' for the communities, was an absolute must, for they also had a strong conviction in the power of his blessings which would, from their perspective, enable them to live happily ever after. I would normally slip in by default as the assistant director of RTU. And then there were those from the housing department led by Lourduswamy, the dynamic and efficient head of that department who excelled in high quality and timely completion of activities. Heads of many other departments were also invited. Ilango and James who looked after education and health programmes respectively, would normally be invited to all such functions since they were an integral part of the team. And so would Rani and Manoba whose mobile clinics had endeared them to those in the surrounding villages.

This was the easier part. The more difficult part was the other invitees, which normally depended on who could potentially contribute to the village development. The other invitees would or could include the local Member of the Legislative Assembly, MLA (if the village tended to support the party s/he represented – they barely thought of inviting the MP as s/he was too distanced from their daily lives). If the MLA was from a party that the village was not supportive of, they would call the local, usually the block level, president of the concerned political party. And then there would be some key administrative officials from the block – the Block Development Officer and his entourage. Getting someone from the district level did not figure high in the priority, though RTU, on a few occasions, did use its contacts to get the District Collector or his/her deputy when requested by the hosting community.

These functions were usually held in the mornings. The arrival of the guests was greeting with the beating of the drums by traditional drummers. As if on cue, some of the more enthusiastic youth would get into an impromptu dance (*tappankoothu*, as they would locally refer to, meaning a casual, joyful way of dancing) and soon, they would be joined by some of their seniors who may have prepared themselves well (a little too well, at times) in advance by gulping in a couple of glasses of the local brew so that they could drop their inhibitions and get into a swinging mood, literally ! The drummers and the dancers would then escort the guests to the place where the function would be held, in some cases, under a small '*pandal*' or marquee. As the guests approached the venue of the function, the guy responsible for the public address system (a critical technocrat on such occasions) would get active by first blowing into the mike or snapping in front of it, with the mandatory '1-2-3 mic testing' repeated usually 3 times, just to ensure that the mic is up and functioning to amplify the greetings of the guests.

The women, in their bright sarees, would have collected as a group nearer to the venue and would ululate excitedly with a great deal of merriment, heightened by the fragrance of the fresh jasmine and '*kanakambaram*' flowers. With their long tresses well oiled and tied in a knot and their bright stone studded nose rings shining brightly in the morning sun, in sharp contrast to their less soberly dressed male counterparts who normally wore white shirts and *dhotis,* except for the youth who would be in brighter coloured shirts and *lungis*. The men's *dhotis* were not all white though. A close look would reveal the *'karai'* or the coloured lines that ran along the horizontal length of the dhoti, and an even closer look could reveal their party preferences. The Dravida Munnetra Kazhagam supporters would prefer wearing *dhotis* with the party's red and black lines along the borders of their *dhotis*. Those supporting the Anna Dravida Munnetra Kazhagam (that broke away from the DMK) would have the same red and black coloured lines on the borders of their *dhotis*, but with a line of white separating the two. The Congress supporters would wear *dhotis* with the Indian tricolour along their *dhoti* borders – saffron, white and green. Some men would make their party affiliations more obvious by draping themselves in a shawl that reflected their party colours or casually placing a small cotton towel on their shoulders which had their party colours.

Coming back to the women, they would now get ready to perform an important function, that of performing the *'arati'* the traditional form of welcome. It normally was done with a plate of water in which vermillion was mixed with a bit of raw rice, leaves and other auspicious items. Holding it in front of their guests, they would move it in around in a clockwise action, take a bit of the solution and apply it on the guests' forehead, and then pour it horizontally in front of the guests for them to step over it. This symbolized protection from evil spirits. I noticed that this was quite different from the north Indian form of *arti* which required a lit oil lamp and which then would continue to be held by the women escorting the guests.

Once the guests were seated at the assigned places (in most cases, the chairs and tables were thanks to the local school !), small plates of *kumkumam* and *chandanam* would be passed around for the guests to apply on their foreheads. Small garlands of welcome would usually follow. And then, one of the village elders would make his way to the mic to formally announce the commencement of ceremonies.

Usually, it started with a prayer song, again, usually sung by children. A bunch of excited kids would make their way to the mic, wearing their best clothes and with neatly combed hair, most of them with a bit of holy ash on their forehead. With wide grins, they would take their position in front of the mic, wave to their parents and friends in the crowd. And then, they would get dead serious. Eyes closed and their faces a picture of concentration, they would start singing the prayers. Suddenly, everything around would be quiet except for the prayer singing. As soon as this was over, the hustle and bustle would begin. People wanting to sit closer to the dais, young chaps running around organizing the snacks, and kids pushing through the spaces to make their presence felt among the adults.

The first speech by the village elder would normally have a long salutation process which would start something like 'The respectful and honourable Bro. Kimpton who has devoted his lives to working for the poor and bringing hope to many, many poor people for over several years........', if translated literally and followed by similar adulatory references to the block officials (some of whom may be visiting the village for the first time in their current tenure). This was followed by the guests being welcomed, one by one, with that gift that I referred to earlier. In most cases, it was a light shawl or a bath towel. As the names of the guests were announced, someone would come up with the shawl or the towel, open it up and wrap it respectively around the shoulders of the guest. In most cases, most of these shawls or towels were returned to the village once the function was over. But shawl or towel, the compere would invariably refer to this piece of cloth as 'ponnadai' which roughly meant the 'golden shawl'. Next, the guests would be invited to cut the ribbon and perform the related functions which would signify the actual inauguration of the housing settlement. And then, the speeches of the guests which mercifully would be short, except when one of the invited block officials with a great love for his own voice would seize the opportunity to publicise his achievements and that of the block he worked in !

Finally, there would be a vote of thanks. But what would mark some of these inaugurations as special was women with new born children running up to Bro. Kimpton (and rarely the other guests !) with a request to bless the child and name him or her. Even though he was British, Bro. Kimpton had a vast repository of names that would seem appropriate. A beautiful girl child, for instance, would be named 'Alageshwari' or the goddess of beauty. A first born male child would normally be named as 'Murugan' or 'Arumugam', the other names of Lord Karthikeya, the son of Lord Shiva and Goddess Parvati, who rode on a peacock and whose most popular abode, the Palani Hill, was not too far from where we were based.

Much more celebration would follow, especially after we and other guests left. The mic sets would continue blaring, more loudly then. There would be meat distributed. Alcohol would flow freely. The frenzied celebrations would continue late into the night after the 'formal inauguration' - and why not ? It was celebrating their move into a more dignified surroundings that they were truly proud of !

25. Ramyabai leads a revolution

The forests were thick and green. The view was indeed breath taking. Small hamlets dotted the landscape. They were really small, rarely more than about 20 houses. In many cases, there were just 3-4 families in a hamlet. It was in one such hamlet in the Ambikapur district of Chattisgarh (then, a part of the central Indian state of Madhya Pradesh) that I met a group of women in late 1994. These were ordinary women from the Korva (tribal) community. But in a sense, they were not so ordinary, if one looked at what they had done to usher in a process of change in their communities.

Conflict had become a way of life for the many *adivasi* (indigenous) families living in this area. And their conflict was with those who were meant to protect the people, maintain law and order and to safeguard the country's rich natural resource. These families were invariably at the receiving end, the victims, and in most cases, for no fault of theirs. The perpetrators were the officials, particularly at the lower level, of the revenue department (which maintained the local land records), the forest department (whose job was to conserve the forests) and the police.

According to these families, they had been living in these forests for as long as they could remember. They were born in these forests. They recollect their parents and other elders talking about these forests as their homes and they as the original inhabitants of these forests. They considered themselves to be the children of these forests. The forests sustained them. It provided them with fruits, roots, leaves, twigs, wood and more importantly, gave them the naturally distilled rainwater for drinking, which flowed through the several small streams. Many of the elders recollected that some of them had lived in the earlier days as just one or two families, moving from place to place, cultivating small patches of land.

Little did they realize that the forests did not belong to them. Long ago, the British had passed laws for the government to control the forest resources, which continued to be followed by the post-Independence, democratically elected governments. The forest policies of the government were geared more to conserve the forests rather than to also consider the livelihoods of those who lived traditionally in the forests and were entirely dependent on these forest for their living. In the eyes of the forest department, these *adivasis* were encroachers on lands on which the government had absolute control.

But their problem just did not end there. Subsequent governments had provided these families with small patches of land, which were considered as 'revenue' land. Which meant, they could live there, and even cultivate small patches of land (even if it hardly yielded anything) to barely eke out a living. But again, unknown to them, these lands had not been effectively converted from being categorized as 'forest' lands to 'revenue' lands. The forest department obviously therefore did not recognize the rights of these *adivasis*, the original dwellers of the forests, to live there. They were, according to the forest department, encroachers, who were a threat to the forest and the environment!

This was something these people could never understand. "How could we ever kill our parents?" they would ask rather innocently. "Likewise, how can we harm the forests, for they are like our parents"! This apparently did not go down well with the forest department. The result was that they were constantly harassed, threatened with eviction and were forced to live an insecure existence. But the officials were also clever. They would never really want these *adivasis* to go away. How else could they get the constant supplies of food, fresh chicken, the intoxicating *mahua* (a flower commonly found in the local forests) brew? How else could they force the women to clean their dwellings, do the household work that would please their wives and also use these women to satisfy their baser instincts ?

A chance meeting with Anil and Utpala sometime in the mid-eighties provided them with a beacon of hope. Anil and Utpala were social workers (or activists, as they were generally referred to). They had seen the poor *adivasis* being exploited. Even the police seemed to be hand in glove with the revenue officials and the forest officials, who wanted to always extract their pound of flesh from these poor families. After all, their area of operation was in the remote forest villages, far away from the eyes of their higher ups. And they were confident that these naïve villagers would never ever muster the courage to complain against them! The fundamental issue that these activists found out was about the improper documentation of their lands, which meant that there was no clarity on who owned how much or who owned which plot of land. It was also not clear if these lands were indeed revenue lands (in which case, these families staying there and cultivating the lands would be legal) or whether they were forest lands (in which case, occupation and cultivation by the villagers would be illegal).

During one of their sojourns through the forests to familiarize themselves with the local issues, the couple reached Bichchalghati, a small hamlet nestling deep in the Ambikapur forests. Initially, the people were a bit surprised to see two strangers coming to their villagers. They were also scared. The only thing they had come to learn about outsiders was that they were exploiters. What have these two come for, they wondered. It did take some effort on the part of Anil and Utpala to build an initial layer of confidence. They tried to explain to them what they intended to do. They wanted to study the local problems, and with the local people, they wanted to work on lasting solutions. They believed that no solution was possible without the people themselves taking initiative and their task was basically to facilitate this process of people coming together and fighting for their rights.

As their visits increased, a certain rapport was built. Confidence grew. There was a very perceptible sense of excitement, especially among the women. The men were cautious. "It all sounds fine to us, but then, these *babus* (government officials) are our *mai-baap* (literally meaning parents, but here, meant to imply 'benefactors'). Fighting for our rights would mean fighting against these *babus*. They will retaliate. How will we withstand that", they often questioned, when there were spirited discussions about confronting the local officials and demanding their legitimate rights. And they knew it very well. Most of them had at least one experience of physical harassment by either the forest officials or the local police. Some had been jailed on charges that they were not clear about ! Some of them were even beaten up for cutting trees on the biding of the local contractor, who also happened to be a very influential local politician. Certainly, enough was enough. They knew that their lives were fraught with risks, that harassment was a common feature and that they would always be insecure.

Enough, was definitely enough, for the women too. Their problems were similar in many ways. They too had suffered at the hands of these officials. They were often taunted and beaten up when they had begged for mercy for their husbands and sons. After a hard day's work, they had, on several occasions, been forced to cook an elaborate meal for one of the local officials, who would also insist that they slaughter their hens which they so preciously had preserved for a special event – a marriage, a festival or for a religious offering. And worse, many of them had been used, abused, their modesty outraged. How could they ever forget the ignominy of the days and nights they were forcibly taken away to the officials' residence or the government guesthouse, only to be subjected to the worst forms of humiliation? Something made them realise that it was now time to act. They had taken it all, lying down. And they had got to a point of 'just no more'!

Dilbar, one of the most vocal women, was the first to respond. "Yes", she said with a steely determination, "yes, we must fight. We have suffered enough. We need to realise that we too are human beings. We too need to be treated with dignity. So what if we are *adivasis*? We aren't animals! If we all come together and stand solidly behind each other, nobody can bring us any harm". Her determination seemed justified. What she said may have seemed a utopian dream at that point in time, but it certainly got the brains of the women ticking. For once, they were willing to throw caution to the winds, much to their husbands' dismay!

Thus began a slow process. The women realized that their strength lay in their numbers. One day, when one of them went to the forests to collect firewood, the forest guard tried to misbehave with her. But she managed to escape and came running to the village. If it had been an earlier time, this incident would have gone unnoticed. At the most, she might have confided in a few women she was close to. But this time, when she narrated the incident to some of the women, they got together in no time. There were 15-20 of them. "We can't allow him to escape this time. Let's go and get him", said Ramyabai, one of the women. Being familiar with the forests, these women tracked him in no time and confronted him.

The forest guard was unapologetic. Though he had been taken aback by the aggression of the women that he had not seen before when he indulged in such a behaviour, he had no inkling of what was in store. His unrelenting attitude angered the women further. One of them had a rope tied around her waist, which was meant to tie the firewood she was supposed to collect. She promptly took out the rope and with the help of the other women, literally 'handcuffed' him, took him to the nearest forest post and handed him over to the forest guard's boss, the ranger. "Mind you, this is a warning", Ramyabai said menacingly, "don't try it ever again". The ranger was taken by complete surprise. He blurted out a quick apology on behalf of his subordinate and asked the women to disperse. That day, they realized that they had achieved something!

But more was yet to come. While they did tackle such individual cases one by one, they were also aware that their confrontation with the forest officials was going to escalate, for there would be retaliation from their side too. After all, the forest officials were more powerful and influential. The women prepared themselves mentally for the worst. Meanwhile, to ensure that there was some security to their livelihoods, they started a savings programme, pinching out a bit from their meagre earnings. Of course, it was not easy. It meant sacrificing on some of their immediate requirements. They also started collecting a small community fund. They were aware that at some point in time, they may have to travel to the district headquarters to meet higher level officials. They were also considering in terms of collecting enough money to engage a lawyer if one of them or their men folk was arrested. It was a small beginning, but then, it had to start somewhere.

One of their constant concerns was about the confusion around the land on which they had built their simple huts with thatched roofs. They just could not understand why they were always threatened with eviction, when apparently, they did not come in anybody's way. Earlier, they could ward off the threat with inducements like the local brew or chicken, or even, in extreme cases, allowing one of the women to serve the officials. But now, they had resolved to claim their rights. There was also a problem regarding their land. The forest officials had always insisted that it was their (read, forest) land and that they had no right to cultivate those lands, that it was illegal and hence subject to eviction. They had earlier experiences when their standing crop was mercilessly burnt down by the forest officials, just days before the harvest, which meant a long season of near starvation! They had gone to the local *tehsildar's* (the revenue official at the sub-district level) office to seek clarification, as repeated assurances of their *patwari* (the village level revenue official responsible for land records and issuing various certificates, to whom they had to pay small sums of money from time to time to lend their lands a semblance of legality!) did not yield any result. The *tehsildar* had initially said that he could nothing about it, but then soon, changed his statement and said that well, he could 'explore' ways, but at a cost. It had meant that each of the families had to shell out Rs. 100 or so for this purpose. As one could imagine, nothing happened. The forest officials continued to threaten them with eviction and destruction of their standing crops. Ultimately, their fate would determine what happened to them, they comforted themselves.

But on discovering the potential of their collective strength, the women had decided to do something about it, though they were not clear what! The time for the test of their determination was to come soon. One day, they heard the sound of a jeep approaching their village. It was not difficult to figure out to whom the jeep belonged. As the jeep screeched to halt, a dozen or so men in *khakhi,* all forest department lower level staffers, got off. The senior most among them, an official they had not met before, led the team. The people heard him being referred to as 'Rana sahib (name changed)'. He surveyed the motley crowd of men, women and children, about 50 or so in all, who had come out of their huts. "What is the matter, *sahib*", one of the men asked meekly. Something was not right, he mused. There was perceptible tension in the air. They had seen and even confronted these officials in ones and twos, but never had they seen such a large team in their village. And some of them were armed, something they did not attempt to undermine. "Get out of your huts, you creeps", Rana shouted to them in general. "You have been told several times that this land does not belong to you. It belongs to us. Enough time has been given. It's time you move now. Take your belongings and get out, right now", he growled. He was a no-nonsense type! "But *sahib*, where can we go now? It's almost evening. We know no other place where we can live. We have been living here for years and have not caused any trouble. Why can't we live here?", one of men asked, very respectfully. "There are small children, old people, pregnant women. Moreover, we have our farms here. Where else can we go and earn a living", he continued to plead.

The officer seemed amused. There was a wicked smile at the corner of his mouth. He came close to Lakha, who had been performing the role of a spokesperson for the group. As he towered over Lakha's frail figure, he said, "You should have thought about it earlier. Unfortunately, of late, you guys have been thinking more about how to corner us and defame us. Some of you, I believe, were also planning to do up to the district level to complain about us. You think we are going to take all this lying down, especially when you have been living here at our mercy"?

The men were visibly scared. There was an uneasy calm. Rana looked around and surveyed the hamlet. There were all mud huts. It wouldn't take too long to demolish these. And the crowd here was pretty manageable too. Rana had a reputation of being ruthless, which these villagers were aware of. He wanted to climb up the hierarchy pretty fast. He knew exactly how to get into the good books of his superiors and the local elite. He had been hearing complaints from his subordinates that these villagers were getting too 'hot' to handle. Apparently, they had formed a '*sangathan*' (association)! The local elite too were not too happy with what was happening. Many of them had migrated from West Bengal several years ago. They could smell a revolution round the corner, which was quite ominous. "Nip it in the bud", they would say.

As Rana contemplated his next move, Ramyabai stepped forward, pushing her way through the men who were standing a little ahead of the women (as would normally be expected). "*Sahib*, we have done no wrong. We have been living here peacefully. What makes you want us to be evicted? Whose orders are you carrying out"? she asked, sternly, yet with restraint in her voice. Her eyes were burning. She could feel the palpitations in her heart. She could not understand where she got the strength to speak out so openly. But she was conscious of the fact that the other women would stand by her. Before Rana could muster a response, the other women chorused, "Yes, she is right. Why should we move? This is our land and we will continue to live here", they said.

Rana was livid. He certainly did not have a reputation for tolerance. And here he was, being challenged by the *adivasis*, and that too, women, who till yesterday, used to dance to his tunes! As he felt a rush of blood through his temples, one of the men pleaded, "*Sahib*, don't listen to her. I beg forgiveness. And I plead that you be considerate enough to allow us to stay here". This time around, it was Ramyabai's turn to get angry. She had not bargained for this, from the men of her community. They could at least have shut up, instead of weakening their resolve! "No", she asserted, "we are not begging for mercy. We are demanding our right to live here".

That was it. Rana caught hold of Ramyabai's hair in a fit of rage and pushed her away with a force that sent her stumbling all the way to where the rest of the women were standing. As she fell to the ground, she looked up to the women and as if on cue, they all surged forward and surrounded Rana. "How dare you treat us like this?" they shouted. "What makes you think you can do anything to us"?

"Get going, you guys! What are you waiting for? Throw the stuff out of their homes and break down their huts. Fast!"

124

Rana barked. He had sensed trouble. But he was equally determined to get his job done. The uniformed men went berserk. Moving from house to house, they systematically broke the fences, and with the butt of their rifles, they brought down the mud walls of the *adivasi* dwellings. They anyway hardly had anything in their homes, but whatever little they stumbled upon, they broke or destroyed mercilessly. There was absolute pandemonium. While some were trying to stop the men from doing further damage and even pleading mercy, some were trying to retrieve or save their frugal belongings. The men in uniform had no mercy. Even the earthen bins used to store grains were destroyed and stamped upon. Some of them even went to the extent of setting fire to the thatch to hasten the destruction.

As the rampaging team receded with loud threats of further harm if they did not move out of their habitation, the villagers turned around to look at the settlement where their simple little huts once stood, their little world now crumbled. All that was left was debris all around. Pots and pans were all over the place. Clothes were strewn. There were small mounds of grain which were destroyed or spilled all over. Smoke emitted from some houses which had been set on fire. It was a sad spectacle. Years of labour and toil had simply been destroyed in the madness that lasted just a few minutes – and for no fault of theirs.

As they sat around, frustrated and humiliated, the only thought that seemed to cross their minds was what would happen next. Would the men come back and cause further damage? Would they also call the police to get them arrested if they physically did not move from there? But the women seemed to be in a different mood. Yes, they were frustrated, yes they felt humiliated, but no, they certainly did not feel diffident or hopeless. They were down, but not out! They knew that their strength lay in their solidarity and were determined to use it to the maximum.

Once again, it was Ramyabai who said, "Let's not sit around, brooding about our fate. It's time for us to unite and fight". The other women nodded. "But it's you who caused it", one of the men said. "What makes you say so", she shot back. "If only you had not been so defiant, we could have been let off with some bribes or chicken or liquor. But now, everything is lost. Do you still want to bring further damage to us"? they asked. "You may say what you want", she continued. "But let me tell you, it's time to fight. If we don't, these guys will get back at us", she said. "What do you want us to do", the men asked. "We will go to the district headquarters and file a complaint with the district level officer", she said. "With the help of Anil and Utpala, we will talk to the journalists and ask them to write about the unfair treatment meted out to us. We can also go and stage a *dharna* (demonstration) in front of the District Collector's office, demanding justice", she said.

The men were quiet. Some of them were clearly cynical. "You think you can do all these? Do you think you can meet the higher-ups? What makes you think they will be better than these fellows? And won't it cost us money to go to the district headquarters and meet other people? And the time that it will take, when we could as well earn some money instead"? they posed. But not all men felt that way. Some of them could see reason. Yes, it meant time, it meant money. Yes, it gave them no guarantee that the reception they would get at the district level would be encouraging. But then, what was the harm in trying? Try they must. "Our women are determined and clear on what they want to do. So, I think it is important we support them instead of being sceptical", they said. Once of them was Lakha.

What happened then was truly amazing, but not easy. Over the next one month, they made several visits to the district headquarters. With Anil and Utpala's help, they met several influential people – from their local Member of Parliament and Member of Legislative Assembly to the District Collector and the District Forest Officer, from lawyers to journalists. Confrontation was fine, they knew. But then confrontation without a critical support base would be meaningless. They had to build allies. They had to know who would support their cause. They had to publicise their cause so that others like them wouldn't face the same fate. They had to keep up the pressure. One message that the women always gave to the men was, "We will be ahead in this struggle. All we need is your backing. Whether it is a *dharna* or a *yatra* (march), we will be in the forefront. All said and done, even the police will not be comfortable reigning blows on us, but they may not hesitate to kick you guys at the slightest pretext. The higher up officials may abuse you, but chances are, they may listen to us. Anyway, whatever happens, we will not buckle. If it means going to the jail, we are prepared. But just don't give up".

As a strategy, it was perfect. *Dharnas, yatras* and *gheraos* (picketing) were resorted to. But never once did any of them indulge in any form of violence. Protests and demonstrations were peaceful. Slogans and songs to build solidarity among themselves emerged. There was a strong bonding, especially since people from the neighbouring villages also joined the cause, for they could be the victims tomorrow!

Obviously, with such well orchestrated action, things could not be hidden further. Articles kept appearing in the local media about how the *adivasis* were being harassed. The Collector and the Superintendent of Police, both of whom happened to be extremely considerate and sympathetic to the cause of the poor *adivasis*, called for further details and explanations. Between them, they also put pressure on the District Forest Officer to act. Even the local MLA, under pressure, was forced to act since elections were not too far away!

After several days of applying pressure, the Collector called them for a meeting to settle the dispute. The Superintendent of Police, the District Forest Officer and several lower level officials were present. The DFO tendered an unconditional apology and assured them that such actions would not be repeated. The Collector also assured them that some public works would be sanctioned for the village so that it could provide additional employment and income for the families and help them recover their loss. He also assured them to look into possibilities of compensating them monetarily for the loss incurred.

It was a significant landmark for the villagers and especially for the women. There was a certain realisation and confidence in themselves that emerged. Suddenly, they realized that they need not always be on the receiving end. They could also influence the way things happened at the local level. It was this realisation that led them to lobby on various other issues. They lobbied actively with the revenue department to get legitimate *pattas* (title deeds) for their lands, subsequent to a government notification that allowed regularisation of *pattas* (for lands that had been occupied by the *adivasis* before October 1980, when the Government's Forest Conversation Policy came into force). At times of drought, they managed to negotiate with the district and block officials to get public works sanctioned for their village. They ensured that the education and health facilities functioned well. It was not just about their rights that they worked on. They realised that they also had a responsibility to co-operate, participate and be engaged, to support government programmes meant for their welfare. And through all these, it was women like Ramyabai who provided the confidence and the leadership they needed!

26. Bairalal and his question

The day long meeting had concluded. It was one of the regular meetings they had periodically. As they got up to leave, they said their usual good-byes. The meeting had been interesting and they always enjoyed this opportunity to meet people from the different villages. But it was also the time when they visited the local market, bought some stuff for their homes that were not normally available in their villages. The end of the meeting was often signalled by a dash to the market. But Bairalal was occupied, deep in thought. His brows were knit. Something surely was troubling him. He lacked the enthusiasm others displayed for their shopping expedition.

This was a monthly meeting of the cluster in-charges nominated jointly by Prayas (a local NGO working in the villages of Chindwada in Madhya Pradesh, central India) and the village communities, somctime in 1995. Local youth, both men and women, had been identified to oversee development initiatives in a group of 5-10 villages, referred to as a cluster, in Prayas' programme area. One of their key functions was to support the village *sangathans* (associations), ensure that the *sangathan* records were maintained properly, that their issues and problems were taken up with the block and district level authorities and to report back to these *sangathans* and to Prayas what needed to be done in these villages. These were fairly remote villages in the Amarwara and Harrai blocks. The population was largely *adivasi* (belonging to the Gond tribe). Decades of exploitation and isolation had impoverished the people of these villages. Prayas had played an important role, from the late eighties, to organise the poor into village *sangathans* and plan development of their respective villages. It had not been easy though with the local authorities and the traders alike resisting the efforts of the people and Prayas to bring about a change that would challenge their erstwhile unquestioned authority and influence they had over these people.

Bairalal had been one of the most outstanding of the cluster in-charges. He was one of the few young men who had managed to get to secondary schooling. He could read and write reasonably well, at least, enough to maintain village accounts, transact small business and write minutes of the village meetings. He was extremely hard working. He toiled in the farms during the day in the agriculture season. Though poor, he had his own dreams of a brighter future. In the evenings, he would set out for his community work. On most days, he would have a meeting in one of the villages that was part of his cluster. If not a meeting, he would be at hand to help the education team with supervising their learning centres, or with the health team spreading health education messages or with the legal aid team helping with organising legal aid camps. He would supervise the grain bank, the seed bank, check the cash savings to ensure that basic systems were followed. He would spend time with individual families, helping them plan for their future. He would resolve conflicts among families or even among villages. A critical function of his was to accompany those in need to the block or district headquarters to follow-up loan applications with the bank or petitions from individuals or communities for some scheme. But more importantly, he would fearlessly walk into police stations or offices of the local forest department officials (something that was quite unthinkable for an *adivasi*, who were more often than not victims of police atrocities or atrocities of the forest department) seeking resolution to the various grievances that his people had or for filing reports against exploitative traders or corrupt officials or simply seeking permission to stage a peaceful protest !

Life was quite busy for Bairalal, but he enjoyed it thoroughly, though his wife often complained about he not attending to pressing needs at home. Bairalal enjoyed it because of the love and respect he gained in the process from his community members. There was a sense of pride and achievement in what he was doing. He had also been recognised by the local officials. More importantly, he felt that he was part of a major change sweeping across the tribal villages of Chindwada, a part of a new assertion, part of creating a tribal or *adivasi* identity that was hitherto suppressed.

Coming back to the day of the meeting, it was a meeting with a difference. Unlike earlier meetings, it was not about assessing progress of work done. This was a forward look meeting. Prayas was preparing a long term plan in consultation with the village communities. I was there to facilitate the process. The long term plan was a strategic plan aimed at visioning where these communities would be in 10 years' time, and what needed to be done in the intermediate period to get there. It was an intensive process with village *sangathans* having long meetings at their level. The perspectives that emerged were then discussed at the cluster-level by the cluster in-charges (Bairlal being one of them), which in turn was consolidated at the level of Prayas and its operational areas.

A good part of the morning was spent on discussing various ideas that had emerged on what needs to be done to bring about all-round development in the lives of the people in the villages. Taking a historical perspective, we started discussing the fundamental causes of poverty and exploitation that the *adivasi* communities found themselves in. That was quite a challenge. Since the cluster in-charges were village youth and did not have the benefit of a long experience and the wisdom that would emerge from being an elder, it was a difficult topic to discuss. The discussion remained inconclusive. But not for Bairalal. The question continued to perturb him. "Why, indeed, were the *adivasis* in the sad condition they were in" ?

It was with this thought that Bairalal left the meeting room, deep in thought and certainly disturbed. Not many of his peers noticed it though Bairalal was often a cheerful, talkative person. The hurry to get to the market and catch the last buses of the evening that would take them to their respective villages were more important. Bairalal remembered that he too had to go to the market. He had promised to buy various things to his wife and he knew it was better that he honour his commitment. But he continued to be lost in thought. So much so that he did not notice Thakur, the local cop who knew Bairalal very well (and why not, with the number of times Bairalal challenging Thakur's authority and actions !). Normally, Bairalal, on his visits, would have a couple of issues to raise with Thakur or his colleagues. But this time, he was very quiet. "Bairalal", Thakur shouted out. "What is troubling you ? Why are you looking lost"? "I need to find a sound answer to a question", Bairalal replied. Thakur guffawed. "And pray, what's that question"? Bairalal turned around, looking directly at Thakur. There was an air of defiance, Thakur felt, in the way Bairalal looked at him. "I need to find out – why are we *adivasis* so poor and exploited"?, he said, turning around and walking away as he completed. It sounded a bit ominous to Thakur. There was a certain sense of determination in Bairalal.

And it is this determination and this questioning that sustained Bairalal's enthusiasm in the face of the several odds that he confronted in his life and work. He was determined to ensure that his community led a better life, were better respected and were better represented in all walks of life. He didn't see any logic or reason on why they should continue to be discriminated against and exploited. And it was people like Bairalal who truly managed to change the way the *adivasis* were perceived in those villages of Chindwada where they worked.

Village *sangathans* grew in strength, their solidarity reinforced with the formation of a federation of these networks. They learnt to be assertive, demanding entitlements that were clearly theirs from the district administration. They developed strong links with various line departments at the district level, with technical resource agencies, the media and even the politicians. They knew that their past was well behind them and they could look to the future with a great deal of optimism for their children to lead a better life !

27. Changing the stereotype

It is experiences like these that convinced me that a silent revolution was sweeping by the countryside, in rural areas, in far flung hamlets and villages. I was once visiting some villages in the Jalaun district of Uttar Pradesh in mid-2003. This was a district which continued to mirror the typical characteristics of a feudal era, where land holding was skewed, where repression of *dalits* and women was marked, the gender ratio was adversely skewed against women, the rates of education especially among the women was very low and the rates of morbidity and mortality were high.

The women I met were members of a self-help group. They had initially started off 4-5 years earlier by saving small amounts so that they could collect a small fund to meet their various needs. Gradually, these evolved as forums for women to look at issues affecting them. They started discussing issues of domestic violence, of sexual harassment while working on the farms of the rich and influential landlords, of the low level of education among the girl children. They started taking part in various village level planning exercises. Some even stood for and got elected into the *panchayats*. They had started insisting on getting their daughters educated. They had negotiated with their men folk to enable women to access more opportunities.

As their work grew, and as the visible impact of their work grew, the men too started taking notice. The men had realized that their women needed to spend more time outside their homes, to visit the block development officer's office, to go to the District Collector's office to press for their demands, to visit the bank in the neighbouring town to deposit their savings etc. They had started getting convinced that these would help them and their villages. As a result, they had started to even undertake domestic chores – taking care of their children, cooking, fetching water and fuelwood etc. which, otherwise, would have been unthinkable in a society steeped in patriarchal culture. The women had also seen the advantage of getting their sons engaged in domestic chores, earlier restricted to the girl children.

While we were discussing these issues, I noticed that many women still had their faces covered. The system of *purdah* was still quite prominent. I asked them about this custom and whether they thought this practice is going to change. "There have been lot of changes over the past 5 years or so. We have started taking various responsibilities and representing the needs of our village with the block and district officials. This never happened before. We have been transacting with the bank. More and more girls are getting educated. We have regular meetings. We speak up in meetings even when our menfolk are around. These are major changes for us. Yes, we still tend to cover our faces when there are other men around. But then, this too, is a matter of time. In a few years from now, even this will disappear", they said emphatically.

I have seen such changes sweeping through many other parts of the country. Our mainstream media, especially our films and television serials, may still be stereotyping our women and glorifying their traditional roles to counter the trend of increased opportunities that women are increasingly seeking, our corporate sector may still be raking in the big bucks by continuing to project women as objects of desire, our cities may be reeling under various atrocities against women, even in the so-called middle and upper class strata, our urban educational institutions and work places may still be a melting pot of sexual harassment .... but these belie a quiet, but significant change that is sweeping across our countryside......!!!

28. The drummers and dancers

It was in one of the villages that Reaching the Unreached (RTU) worked in, that we found a professional group of drummers. It was in the early '90s. These drummers belonging to a particular caste group had once approached RTU for supporting a housing programme. They had been allotted land by the state government, about 3-5 cents (100 cents make an acre) but had no money to build a decent house. What they did have was small huts, the walls of which were made of mud and the roof was thatched. The 40 odd families there were all landless labourers. The only other skill they had was their drumming (with some playing other musical instruments to keep the drums company). Their income from drumming came during the brief festival season which normally was post the winter harvest in January and would go on till about May. Or else, they would once in a while, be invited for some political function or such other events.

The income from drumming was meagre. A group of about a dozen drummers would make just about Rs. 500 for a performance. Incidentally, the drummers were also good dancers, and that is what added a certain charm to their drumming. They had a repository of synchronized steps which would change each time they changed the rhythm with which they beat their drums. Normally, a group of six men would stand facing another group of six men, rhythmically playing their drums. Gradually, they would move forward, cross each other, turn around and face each other again from their new positions. At times, they would form a circle with the main drummer getting into the middle. The patterns they made with their drumming was quite fascinating. As the drumming progressed, they would get into a frenzy with the drums reaching a crescendo, that would make the stiffest and lead footed among those in the crowd to get into the swing. Suddenly, they would bring down the pace of the drums, starting from a low pace and gradually build up. It was said that they had the stamina to dance all night, though I could not witness that. What I did see was their performance which lasted for about a couple of hours. Strangely, they seemed to be in a mood to go on and on, though the onlookers looked tired due to the occasional jig they got induced to performing with the beats of the drums.

Drumming was serious business for them, in spite of all the joy and frenzy with which they performed. The more the onlookers enjoyed their performance and broke into dancing, the more encouraged they would be. All they wanted in between was some bottles of the local soda or the 'colour', though it was often said that they would gulp down a few glasses of the local brew to give them the stamina to keep going. Most of the drummers were young men below thirty, though they were commanded by someone more senior, who was the one who sought drumming assignments, collected the cash and distributed it amongst the troupe members. They all had a certain uniform which was white long sleeved shirt and white trousers, adorned by red and golden patterns. Their drums were also attractively coloured. The drummers of Singarakkottai – that is how they were referred to, named after the village where they lived. Though they were on the main state highway connecting the towns of Batlagundu and Dindigul, they were stricken by poverty, none of which was of course evident when they performed.

They were once spotted by the local authorities to perform as part of the opening ceremonies for the Asian Games (Asiad) held in New Delhi in 1982. Though it was a decade since then, they could never stop sharing the excitement they had of traveling to Delhi, experiencing the different weather, culture and food there and the opportunity to meet 'Amma', Mrs. Indira Gandhi, the then Prime Minister of India, who had hosted a reception for the performers from various states who had been mobilized to make the opening ceremony a memorable one. They had witnessed the *dandia raas* from Gujarat, the *lavni* from Maharasthra, the *bhangra* from Punjab, the bamboo dance from Manipur, the *panchavadyam* from Kerala. It was an amazing experience. They had mingled with these artistes in spite of their limitation of not knowing Hindi at all (thanks partly due to their lack of education and the fact that Hindi was barely spoken, taught or used in Tamil Nadu. Remember, this was well before the invasion of Bollywood and the *saas-bahu* soaps offered by a plethora of private television channels !). But what they discovered which intrigued them was though there seemed to be a wide appreciation of their art form, artistes like them lived in penury and were eking their livelihood through various other forms, mostly related to casual labour. In a way, they had felt a strange sense of oneness and solidarity with those artistes on discovering that most of them went through similar problems in life.

The Singarakkottai inauguration to mark the completion of the low-cost housing project for this community was therefore significantly different. In addition to everything else that we witnessed in other villages, there was this absolutely fascinating performance by the drummers, which led most of the guests to shed their stiffness and inhibitions of being 'VIPs' and get on with their dancing instead. It was a great sight. Being on the roadside, most passing vehicles halted to view this wonderful sight. It was like a festival bursting out in the countryside at a time when no festivities were scheduled, for it was neither a traditional festival season, nor was it a wedding season ! Since then, the Singarakkottai drummers were a regular group for all RTU celebrations. It was a special relationship that they built. Their popularity soared with each subsequent performance and we hoped this did, in some small way, help to hone their skills and induce them to invest in improving their skills further - and more importantly, to keep that art form alive !

The other performing art that we had got used was 'Oyilattam' performed by the villages of Dharmalingapuram, a small village of about 50 families of the Naicker caste situated on the main Batlagundu- Periyakulam road. We got to enjoy whenever there was any function in the village, mostly related to the events in the school, as it was a treat watching their Oyilattam. It was performed by the men of the village. A couple of them would sing to which the rest of the men, about 6 to 8 in the age group of 16-40 would dance. Standing in a line, wearing white shirts and *dhotis*, with a red scarf tied around their waist and with *ghunghroos* tied at their ankles, they would sway with rhythmic synchronization, waving a handkerchief as their arms moved in tune with the dance steps. The Oyilattam, for them, was much more than a dance. It was a way for them to get together and reinforce the solidarity of their community, for which they were known. The songs often reflected various aspects of their culture, beliefs and ways of life.

What was common between the Singarakottai drummers and the Oyilattam of Dharmalingapuram was that these were performed exclusively by the men - and as with many other performing arts, these were as much a way of life as it was part of their culture and tradition. And both were suffering from the similar fate - a ebbing of interest in their respective art forms due to the onslaught of cinema and TV, forcing them to abandon this art and look for other means of livelihood !

29. The *basti* transforms !

It was not yet summer. Towards the end of March (this is 2012), it is still supposed to be spring time. But by the time we got to the Bajrangnagar community in Indore, it was quite warm and the hall which was the venue of our meeting with the community was packed, mostly by women. We had come to meet this community as part of the WaterAid team, where our partner NGO, BGMS (Bhartiaya Grameen Mahila Sansthan) had been working for several years on various community development initiatives. It was an organization formed by women for women, but their work benefited the entire community, and the children in particular.

"I came here because I had fallen in love with a young man from this community and got married to him. But when I came here to live after my marriage, I wondered if I had been stupid to do so" said Sunita, rather nonchalantly ! There was considerable mirth around her frank confession. "This was quite sometime back. I lived in a reasonable neighbourhood but I was appalled by the conditions that people lived in. The worst thing was that there were no toilets. I was not used to relieving myself in the open – and that was very difficult for me to come to terms with. But I realized that at that time, I did not have an alternative ! That is when I decided to work with BGMS team and see what I could do to support development here. During this period, I studied hard, got my degree, completed my post graduation and am now working as a teacher. But I am still involved with BGSS on a voluntary basis" she said.

It was a fascinating story of change. From being a typical slum over two decades ago, with support from BGSS, the community had succeeded in transforming the settlement from a lowly slum to a well developed community, pretty much like a middle class settlement. Houses had been renovated, there were good cement-and-concrete roads, drains were well laid out and overall, it was quite clean compared with the general standards of cleanliness that one would expect to see in a similar neighbourhood in an Indian city.

Sunita's personal testimonial became a trigger for many women to narrate their own stories and experiences. The narrative was quite similar – they had been contacted and encouraged by BGMS, the BGMS team came and trained them to be community workers, they mobilized women in their neighbourhood, savings were collected, loans were given, life had changed and they are now looking forward to a much brighter future for their children. Women from different communities in the city of Indore, with different backgrounds, many from the *adivasi* community called the Bhils, had migrated to the city in search of livelihoods from the rural hinterland that was affected by drought and failing agriculture or related livelihoods.

Through all this, one of the women, who must have been in her mid-fifties, listened intently. She appeared to be in no mood to speak, but seemed to listen intently, perhaps reliving for herself her own past life in the community. Dressed in a blue sari with her head covered, the stories that other women were saying seemed to resonate with her. She was nodding in agreement, smiling occasionally, but sitting very quiet. And suddenly, she raised her hand, indicating her intention to speak. And speak, she did – her story and what she had seen and experienced.

"My name is Vasanti Jodha. I am from the Bhil community. I came here several years ago. I had 3 children then and the youngest one was just a few days old. The situation here was horrible. From the main road, we had to balance ourselves on a log of wood to cross a dirty stream into which all waste, human and solid waste, was emptied. The sight was disgusting, the stench was awful. It was quite a task to balance ourselves on the log of wood as we tried to cross the stream without falling. Many children had fallen, some died, some were wounded. But that was the only way in which we could access our settlement. All the houses were temporary in nature, built with bamboo poles and draped with rags, jute bags or anything that we could lay our hands on. The whole place was dirty. Children were regularly falling ill."

"No one cared for us. On the contrary, we were victims of anything that happened in the city. If there was a burglary, the police would come looking for us as if we were responsible for any crime in the city. When the police came, we had to run for cover – as we didn't know whose husband, brother or son was going to be arrested. They would be gone for days and we would not know what fate awaited them. We were considered as dirty, unwelcome people, petty criminals. When we went to the local office of the municipality to ask for support for some jobs, health or education, we were shooed away. But a few weeks before the elections, once in every five years, we would have politicians coming in asking for votes, saying that all our problems would be sorted. We used to wonder – how come they are discovering us now. Where were they all these years ? Falling into the trap of their promises, we would vote for those who we seemed to trust. And once elected, we would go to greet the successful candidate – only to be shooed away again. 'Sahab is busy' we were told 'and he cannot meet you'. Well, he came to ask for votes, we voted for him, so why would he not see us, we often wondered. But we thought that was our fate and we were destined to live a life like this – neglected, wretched and poor".

"And then, we had the team from BGMS. When they came, we thought that they too were like any other outsider, coming in for their own gains. We had many people coming here offering us various things and making all kinds of promises and we had learnt not to trust them anymore. Why would BGMS be different ? In fact, we would avoid them. But they persisted. They kept coming back and saying that we need to work together to solve our problems. They started talking to us about education, why we should educate our children. They wanted our children to be immunised. Since they were all women, they would speak to the women and ask them to get organised. They encouraged us to save a little so that we could revolve it amongst ourselves when in need. They offered us small loans. Slowly, things started changing."

"Some of us started small businesses – vegetable and fruit vending, tailoring, small livestock, small scale trading. Initially, our husbands wondered what we are up to. We were scolded and ridiculed for spending time in meetings. But when they started seeing the results, they realised that we were doing something very important. Gradually, we started looking at issues of cleanliness and of waste. Our settlement was very dirty. There were no toilets. Water supply was completely lacking. We were fetching dirty water from nearby sources or buying it which was very expensive. What BGMS did was to take us to the municipal corporation to demand water supply and support for construction of toilets. It was not easy. We kept going regularly. We asked them to come to our settlement and see our conditions".

"Eventually, things started happening. They came and saw our problems but also saw that there was so much self-help happening through women's groups. We said we would contribute to the water project, which we did. We also said that we will ensure that it is well maintained and that we paid our dues on a regular basis. We were also granted support for construction of toilets".

"This led to an increase in our confidence. We started going to the municipal corporation on our own without BGMS. We negotiated with them on waste collection. A system was put in place because of which solid waste is collected every day. Under the programme for urban development, we negotiated and eventually were granted a project to build cement and concrete roads in our neighbourhood. All this further increased our confidence. Women started doing more for their own livelihood. They grew their businesses. We now have reasonable incomes to take care of our families or make a big contribution to our family income. We also have a woman building contractor (pointing out to a woman about her age sitting nearby) who started by building toilets after getting trained in basic masonry skills. Now she constructs houses – she has also taken up contracts for building two-storeyed houses in this and other settlements". You could sense the vicarious pride that Vasanti experienced narrating this last bit !

"We were poor and living with no dignity. But today, we are respected. People come to visit us. Officials and politicians listen to us. The police cannot harass us any longer. We may still be poor, but we feel confident and empowered. And we do feel confident that our children will never see the days that we have, will never experience the vulnerability and indignity that we faced!".

30. The quiet curiosity

This was in one of the villages near Thiruvananthapuram in Kerala in late 2004. Some of us, that included some people from Andhra Pradesh working with the state government, were visiting women's groups supported under the Government of Kerala's highly acclaimed programme, the Kudumbashree programme. These groups had engaged in various activities for their economic development. The group we were visiting belonged to the Dalit community. An interaction with them had been organized in the rather spacious and well maintained panchayat building.

At the appointed time, a group of about 15 women assembled in the hall. They were all neatly dressed. From their physical appearance, no one could possibly believe that they were poor. But their sense of self-esteem was striking. Each one had a note pad and a pen, ready to take notes on any useful points that may emerge from the discussions. They needed only a one-way translation. While the visitors asked questions in English which they could easily follow, they replied in Malayalam which I translated into English for the visiting group.

After a series of questions from the visitors which were very articulately responded to, one of the visitors said, "It is quite impressive to know that you all are well educated, in spite of your poverty. You dress so well that it's so difficult for us to even think about yourselves as being poor. You are able to communicate very well. But there is one difference between you and the rural women of Andhra Pradesh. The poor women there do indeed look poor, are not able to communicate in any language other than Telugu and are not able to dress as well as you do. But they are certainly much more vocal that you are. You are a much quieter lot, responding only to the questions we ask".

The women giggled. They found the comparison quite amusing. One of them, Geetha, who seemed to be one of the youngest in the group, then said, "Sir, we do have questions and we would have been more vocal. But we were told that you have limited time and that we should spend time in explaining to you our programme. Hence we didn't ask you anything. But if you have the time, we would like to ask you a few questions". Our friend from Andhra Pradesh beamed. He was happy that he had been able to get them to participate more actively. "Sure, go ahead. We can certainly spend more time talking to you". What followed then was a volley of questions that took us all by surprise. Some of the questions were :

"What is the role of information technology in economic development of your state"?
"How have the rural poor, and especially women, benefited from the Information Technology boom that is so often mentioned in the context of Andhra Pradesh"?
"We hear that farmers in Andhra Pradesh commit suicides. If your state is developing so well, why are farmers being affected"?
"How do you ensure that rural producers are able to benefit from the market, which normally is controlled by the rich"?

We were taken by surprise, to say the least. The level of education and awareness was reflected so clearly through the sharp questions they had raised. So what if they were *Dalits* or if they were poor ? They had kept themselves abreast of developments in other parts of the country. Needless to mention, our group did find it difficult to answer these questions to their satisfaction. But as hosts, the women were gracious enough not to grill us too much !

31. Where are they ?

It was a hot May afternoon in 2013. Returning to Hyderabad after several years, I could sense how this city had grown immensely, just going by the heavy traffic and the general buzz around the city – a city that had prospered in the modern era thanks to the IT boom. Cyberabad was an alternate name to the city.

But the main arterial roads do not tell the full story – and that is what we got to know from Chandbhai, one of the volunteers of *Basti Vikas Manch*, a local community forum of people (loosely translated as Neighbourhood Development Forum) living in low income settlements or *basti* of Bhokalpur. Their origins had an interesting yet tragic beginning.

The local community, who were supplied water through a network of pipes by their local utility were rudely awakened when contaminated water killed 30 people in a matter of few days in 2009. Till then, people were largely concerned about getting just about enough water in their locality. Little did they realise that this very water could one day be the cause of a major tragedy. The reason was that there was a sewer pipe that was running just above the water pipe, and leaks in both these pipes resulted in the water being contaminated.

30 deaths in a matter of a few days was indeed shocking, but the apathy of those responsible was even more so. When the local community members went to complain, they found that neither the officers of the water utility nor their local elected representatives in the municipality were available. In a desperate act, they lodged a 'missing report' with the local police station, expressing concern for their officers and elected representatives who had gone 'missing'. Thanks to some sympathetic journalists, they were also able to get media

attention to a tragedy that could otherwise have gone unnoticed.

This terrible experience resulted in several positive benefits. Firstly, the local community decided that they had to be organised and that they could not simply rely on their elected representatives who had other vested interests. *Basti Vikas Manch* was a result of that realisation. A community that had a significant representation of both Hindus and Muslims and in a context that could potentially be sensitive and vulnerable to communal violence, it was important that local interests were way above narrow religious ones.

Secondly, the importance of safe water became very apparent. Water quality monitoring became important. They set up local labs with basic equipment to ensure regular testing of water quality. With a strong community forum, water supply was being monitored, but water quality monitoring was also given equal importance.

Thirdly, the community also realised the importance of proper sanitation facilities. Now this was a major challenge given the congested settlement. During my visit, they shared a new problem – a public toilet was demolished as those living near the toilet complained about stench. And while the men had the option of using the toilets of a mosque nearby, for the women, there was a serious concern about lack of facilities yet their needs were not recognised or addressed.

Things had then significantly improved, thanks largely to the dedicated work of the volunteers, cutting across social and economic groups in the community to ensure that people had access to water. Sanitation as a challenge was being addressed. But more importantly, their voice and organisation had been recognised by the local utility, who then urged them to come to them directly with their complaints before reporting it to the local media, a tactic they had used effectively in the past. It was not surprising therefore that the level of responsiveness of the service providers has significantly increased !

32. Epilogue

These stories from over three decades of my life have a strange way of refreshing memories that have always been part of me, but stored somewhere deep in my subconscious. Perhaps that is because I was always one for nostalgia. But then, in a different way, it also brings me back to a life that one yearns for, and one knows will never come back to you. These experiences have enriched me so much. These have shaped my thoughts and perspectives and made me appreciate the power of resilience. These stories have entertained me and inspired me. These have made me feel connected and believe in the power of the human spirit.

I only hope that I can continue to find more of these stories and that these continue to enthuse and energise me. In a world that is troubled by conflict and climate change, not to mention the Covid pandemic, I hope we continue to be inspired by stories of courage and resilience as we aspire for a world that is more safe, more just and more equal.

Printed in Great Britain
by Amazon

79124951R00088